High and Wide

When Grief and Love Collide

Carol,
In loving memory of your dear
husband Phil.
May you experience comfort,
healing, hope + joy.
Love Nadine Sands
xox

by Nadine Sands

"And may you have the power to understand, as all God's people should, how wide, how long, how high, and how deep His love is."

Ephesians 3:16 (NLT)

Published by Sails Up Publishing, October, 2019
ISBN: 9780995334625

Editor: Melanie Saxton
Typeset: Greg Salisbury
Book Cover Design: Janine Boudreau
Title Hand Lettering: Jeannine Lode
Portrait Photographer: Warin Marie Photography

DISCLAIMER: This book has been created to inform individuals with an interest in ALS. It is not intended in any way to replace other professional health care or mental health advice, but to support it. Readers of this publication agree that neither Nadine Sands, Michael Sands nor their publisher will be held responsible or liable for damages that may be alleged or resulting, directly, or indirectly, from their use of this publication. All external links are provided as a resource only and are not guaranteed to remain active for any length of time. Neither the publisher nor the author can be held accountable for the information provided by, or actions resulting from accessing these resources. All opinions in this book are those of the author.

Citations

For my mom and dad:

I am so grateful for their steadfast love and faithful prayers.
Their devotion to each other, to their family, and to serving
the Lord has been a gift to witness.

For my family and friends
and everyone who has loved and lost:

May you know personally the comforting, healing, redeeming
power of God's love; His high and wide, King-sized love!

Testimonials

In her book, reflecting on her husband's battle with ALS and then his passing, Nadine reveals that not only is God bigger, but God is enough. When one chapter in life closes, another one is beginning to be written. It would be easy to gloss over the hard parts of ALS, but Nadine wades through them honestly and comes out the other side somewhat weary, but stronger—even enlightened. Nadine models how to move forward without forgetting, how to live while honouring the first love of her life, and how to use what was painful in her life to help others through their own trials.

This book shows that life is both joy and pain, victory and defeat, and disappointment and surprise. It also shows us that maximizing every moment and cherishing every memory is the secret to making it through. In the end, love prevails both human and divine, and is the only suitable answer to the tragedies life too often brings.
Dr Tom Blackaby, Author, Pastor, International Speaker

Nadine takes her readers on a vulnerable journey in her first book, Hold On, Let Go, Facing ALS with Courage and Hope. *She sheds light on how grief enlarges the heart to love with greater depth and compassion. I was in awe of how she and Mike did their sacred dances each day in the midst of great pain and suffering. Now, in her new book,* High and Wide, *Nadine shares about her new love, Chris, and their deep, intimate connection. Yet, the greatness of their love does not diminish what she had with Mike, nor does it gloss over her grief. Her loss left a void that is not filled in by another love, but in a strange way, enhances her love with Chris.*

Nadine's story liberates others and leads them down paths of hope for their own stories. She quotes CS Lewis when describing the journey of love God has taken her on: "Grief is like a long valley, a winding valley where any bend may reveal a totally new landscape." Nadine invites her readers into her different emotional landscapes and we have much to glean from her life story, which she describes as "living hopefully, joyfully and courageously with a big lump in her throat."

As a woman who has lived with my own grief of losing a husband and a son to cancer, I can honestly say, Nadine's sensitivity and honesty in both of her books helps navigate the way through a dark valley, giving us hope that treasures can truly be found even on the darkest of days.

Dana Goodman, Author of *In the Cleft: Joy Comes in the Mourning*, Grief Counsellor

I devoured Nadine's first book, Hold On, Let Go. *I couldn't put it down, and then lent it to many friends. I fervently read this book and Nadine's wisdom, once again, made a huge impact on me. She eloquently beckons, "Go ahead, get your hopes up," even in grief and loss. With that, I was given permission to be hopeful. Wow! A true epiphany for me! And that's how she writes—bam! Time and time again throughout, I was thrown off guard with her messages that make complete sense. I kept asking myself,* Why didn't I think of that? *When we are struggling and feeling heart wrenching pain, doesn't it make sense to learn from someone who also has struggled?*

I am thrilled to have Nadine as my teacher, motivator and guide in my own grieving experiences. Continuously giving God the glory, she repeatedly gains refreshment and strength from Him.

Thank you, Nadine, for sharing a courageous message of love and hope.

Karen Harmon, Author of *Looking for Normal*, Education Assistant, Fitness Instructor

When you're looking for wisdom, it's important to hear from those who have gone before you. Nadine has walked through grief and experienced love. Her book is a guide to finding hope through life's challenges that we all face in different ways. It is written with a refreshing level of honesty that speaks directly to your life. I highly recommend this book!

Andy Steiger, Author, Pastor, President of Apologetics Canada

Contents

Citations III

Dedication V

Testimonials VII

Foreword XIII

Introduction XV

Chap 1: Big Fat Lies, Beautiful Thighs and World Peace 1

Chap 2: High Hopes and Anchor Ropes 19

Chap 3: It's OK. Judge my Book by Its Cover 37

Chap 4: Ahoy, Matey—So Long, My Friend 49

Chap 5: Spaghetti and Words That Make You Squirm 63

Chap 6: Don't Quit and Remember Your Deodorant 77

Chap 7: My Other Sheila with the Gift of Gab and a Great Laugh 89

Chap 8: A Little Bird Sometimes Falls to the Earth, but God Sees Her 97

Chap 9: God's Sovereignty and the Importance of Fresh Breath 115

Chap 10: Dark Clouds, Lemon Drops and Diamonds in the Rough 127

Chap 11: The Most Beautiful Mayday Since 1948 145

Chap 12: Gluten-Free Pancakes and a Lost Girl Like Me 163

Chap 13: Best Friends & PALs and Laying your Burdens Down 177

Chap 14: Love in Photographs and a First Dance 193

Chap 15: Must Love God and Stepdaughters and Stepsons 207

Chap 16: Good News of Great Joy and My Love for Squats and Lunges 227

Chap 17: The Sky's the Limit and the Story Isn't Over Yet 243

Chap 18: The Best is Yet to Come, and What Grief and Cherry Blossoms have
          in Common 257

Acknowledgements 279

Author Biography 283

Foreword

I read Nadine's first book *Hold On, Let Go* in the midst of caring for my wife who was living with Alzheimer's disease. Nadine's book was incredibly impactful. More than any book I had read before, I found myself writing down quote after profound quote that personally spoke to me and encouraged me. Her insights reminded me of God's love and faithfulness. Those reminders were necessary for me to remain effective in loving my wife to the end of her earthly journey and beyond.

After my wife relocated to her heavenly address, God blessed me with the friendship of another very godly woman, Donna (who I've started calling Dee). Dee is a good friend of Nadine's who also lost her husband to ALS. Dee was reading Nadine's manuscript when we met. Since then, Dee and I fell in love and got married, and during that time read the manuscript of this book together (a pre-proofread). We couldn't put the book down. We wept often as the beauty of God permeated our hearts through Nadine's writing. She mirrored our journey of caregiving—experiencing similar pain, passion, confusion, joy, sadness, grief, love and loss while serving and trusting Jesus. As Nadine shared her soul with us through these pages, she wrote as a cherished friend might. Her vulnerability was like therapy to us. And her writing paralleled our version of When grief and love collide. We repeatedly exclaimed, "That's us! That's us, too!"

There are so many great stories contained in these pages. They are all moving, but some perhaps random. I began thinking, *But what is Nadine's main point of this book? What is the thread that weaves throughout everything written in the book? What is it that wraps around and binds it all together?* Two things immediately came to my mind. Her heart and God's heart both reflect Divine love. Her heart of love saturates every story, every relationship, every pain, every thought and every perception. And in the midst of it all, she points all her readers to our Heavenly Father's heart of love. He is honoured on every page as you observe Him orchestrating and bringing all His beautiful manifestations of love to our attention, even in, what many would have perceived, ugly places.

Nadine's writing reflects how she views every aspect of her life in light of the following passage: "Summing it all up, friends, I'd say you'll do best by filling your minds and meditating on things true, noble, reputable, authentic, compelling, gracious—the best, not the worst; the beautiful, not the ugly; things to praise, not things to curse. Put into practice what you learned from me, what you heard and saw and realized. Do that, and God, who makes everything work together, will work you into his most excellent harmonies." Philippians 4:8 (Message).

That is how Nadine writes. Yes, there have been difficult and dark times all along her journey, but she's focused so wonderfully on the beautiful in the midst of it all. Indeed, she has put that heavenly attitude, mindset and lifestyle into practice as instructed in the above passage.

Jory Mitchell, Public School Teacher, Speaker for the Alzheimer Society, Vancouver Coastal Health and University of British Columbia.

Introduction

"To everything there is a season, a time for every purpose
under heaven..."
Ecclesiastes 3:1 (NKJV)

The decision to bury or to flush that first dead goldfish can be
a tough one. And so, the letting go and the grieving begins. As
we make room in our hearts for things we love, we learn very
quickly about grief and loss.

They say grief is the price we pay for love. We actually give
Queen Elizabeth ll credit for saying those exact words, but
even prior, British psychiatrist Dr. Colin Murray Parkes said,
"The pain of grief is just as much part of life as the joy of love:
it is perhaps the price we pay for love, the cost of commitment."

Who knows who actually said it first, but it's a concept we
learn at an early age whether we can verbalize it or not. Shortly
after birth, we're introduced to death. Nature itself is a lesson
on the fleetingness and fragility of life with the changing leaves
on trees and little crawly things. Perhaps God gave us goldfish
and hamsters to gently ease us in.

The losses as we grow and get older, increase. Do we avoid
love so we can avoid grief? Some do, but most of us continue
to love and become more and more familiar with the pain that
comes from loss.

I personally never had a goldfish, but up until my early
forties I had what I would consider typical grief experiences.
I lost a dog and other pets, grandparents, uncles and aunts
and even a couple of friends, but on March 7, 2011 when I

heard the words amyotrophic lateral sclerosis (ALS) for the first time, I was immediately inducted into a twenty-four-hour, seven-day-a-week world of grief. It was the beginning of the letting go process of the closest person to me—my beloved husband Michael, who was diagnosed with the incurable illness, otherwise known as Lou Gehrig's Disease.

After the initial shock wore off, Mike's strong faith in God enabled him to quickly find contentment and peace in the face of death. I was so inspired and moved by his continued positive attitude, his wonderful sense of humour and his courage.

That is what inspired me to start my blog called ALS With Courage. My posts were a great way to keep friends and family informed of Mike's constantly changing condition. It also allowed me to reveal his incredible spirit. Over time though, it became so much more than that—a ministry for others and therapy for me. It also became a collection of lessons, including the lesson of letting go.

Mike let go of working, walking, talking, eating, moving, and slowly he let go of breathing. And slowly I let go of him.

During the last eight months of Mike's life, I wrote a book about our lessons of letting go titled *Hold On, Let Go - Facing ALS with Courage and Hope*. It's a "stay positive in difficult times" kind of story. It's also, and ultimately, a love story. It leaves off where this book starts.

High and Wide is the four-year journey of grief and healing proceeding the earthy farewell of Mike. During this time, I also had to say goodbye to my mom and some other loved-ones and, to my surprise, was faced with the decision to open my heart and let the love of another man inside. I've learned the journey of grief and love is a never-ending and ever-expanding one.

Like my first book, *High and Wide* includes passages from my blog. It's my personal roadmap of unending love that goes above and beyond the limits of this worldly existence. It's for anyone who has loved and lost and for anyone who has ever felt unloved and lost. This may be posing the obvious, but isn't that most of us, if not all of us?

By the way, it's not necessary to read my first book to understand this one. It stands on its own and I hope it blesses you on the journey you're on.

CHAPTER 1
Big Fat Lies, Beautiful Thighs and World Peace

"We love because He first loved us."
1 John 4:19 (NIV)

Sometimes it's hard to know where to start. For instance, this book. I have a title and a lot of content and I think I even have an ending, but I've been wondering where on earth do I start? It's like when you run into someone you haven't seen in a long time and they ask how you've been. Or you go to your high school reunion and people ask what's new with you. It's like, ummm, where do I start? Well, I could start in a hundred different places, but speaking of high school reunions, I'll start right here…

My Big Fat Awesome Legs - Nov 20, 2015

You might read the title of this post and think it sounds pretty superficial in light of what's going on in the world these days. But I hope you will read and discover it might actually have a little something to do with world peace.

I'm an education assistant. At work the other day, while out on the playground at recess, a little girl came

1

up to me very upset about something a boy said. "He told me I'm not a girl," she explained, hurt and confused and embarrassed.

I immediately got down to her level and huddled her and her friend under my umbrella like we were a team discussing the next play. I looked her straight in the eye and told her how preposterous it was for anyone to think she wasn't a girl. Well, I didn't say it exactly that way, but she immediately stopped crying. Then I told her something every girl should learn at her age.

"He made that ridiculous comment because he probably likes you." Then I added, "Don't take it personally, girls." The "personally" part might have gone over their heads, but happily they both ran off. As they left, I said it again a little louder, "Don't take it personally girls!" And under my breath, I continued, "You are strong, you can do anything, you've got this!"

I was able to share something with these little girls that I didn't learn until I was older. Not even in high school, but at my high school reunion, I learned this valuable and heartbreaking lesson: the boy who tormented and teased me from about grade four right up until high school graduation, the boy who rode his bike up and down my street making fun of me about my weight and other things, really LIKED me. *What?*

Let's call him "Jay." Jay glommed on to me right away at that ten-year high school reunion nineteen years ago, and followed me around like a lost little puppy. It was kind of cute at first but became annoying very quickly. Eventually, I asked him why he was following me and being so nice after tirelessly taunting me for all the years we were in school together. He confessed it was because he liked me.

"I had a huge crush on you," he said.

Honestly, I could have strangled him. I could have punched Jay right in the face, but by God's grace I was able to cut him some slack. Looking back, there were other "teasers" too. Like they say, kids can be cruel, and I wasn't always an angel either. Plus, Jay didn't start those thoughts; those thoughts came into my life before he did. He just drilled them home. He just confirmed my ugly childhood feelings about my "ugly" self. I never shared those feelings with anyone. Instead, I stuffed them away, pretending I was okay. Oddly enough, I often stuffed them down even further with food as I began my journey of on-again, off-again dieting.

At the age of eight or nine, you hear a little faint voice for the first time saying, "Your legs are bigger than hers." The whisper gets louder. "Not only are you fat, you're kind of dumb." Eventually the voices scream, "YOU ARE WORTHLESS!" And unfortunately, these words become labels over us.

The yo-yo dieting and self-loathing became routine for me and one constantly enticed the other. It's funny because I had words of encouragement from home and elsewhere, but the negative words, for some reason, spoke louder. I believed the lies because, I guess, I wasn't buying into my Heavenly Father's vast love for me. Even to this day, I struggle to believe He loves me the way He does, just the way I am. The dieting is over (for the most part) and the self-loathing is gone too, but God continually tries to get this through: "I love you the way you are." And I still find it so hard to accept.

I still sit in the bathtub sometimes and wonder if I should cry over the size of my thighs or over the fact that I'm so vain. Should I be upset that I'm still not "good enough" or that, unlike me, so many people don't have strong legs, hot water to bathe in, a roof over their heads, food to eat, or safety? Wow, perspective can weigh a ton.

I'm convinced the mess in our heads and in this world exists because we can't grasp how wide and long and high and deep our Father's love is for us. It could be argued that it's simply sinfulness. But think about Adam and Eve and how pure they were. They'd never been teased or labeled unworthy, yet they still couldn't grasp the love of God and trust Him fully. Instead, they did it their own way. And here we are today, still doing it our own way, unable to grasp His love and trust Him without reserve.

The voices say, "You are ugly. You are fat. You're dumb. You're a disgrace." God says in Psalm 139, "I knit you together in your mother's womb and you are fearfully and wonderfully made." The voices say, "You make the same mistakes over and over again, and when will you ever learn?" God says in Lamentations 3:23, "My mercies are new every morning." He promises in 1 John 1:9, "If you confess your sins, I am faithful to forgive you." He assures us in Isaiah 43:25, "I blot out your sins and remember them no more."

He also says, "I knew you in the secret place; you are not a mistake. Your name is on the palm of my hand. I know when you sit and when you stand; My thoughts about you outnumber the grains of sand. My plans for you are filled with hope. I am with you wherever you go. You are the apple of my eye and I rejoice over you with singing. I've loved you from the beginning and there is no end to my love. I love you as far as my Son, Jesus, could stretch out His arms. His sacrifice on the cross was my way to display my extravagant love for you and amazing grace."

Regarding the "teasers" and the "bullies," you know what they say: "Hurt people hurt people." They also say something about fear, not hate, being the enemy of love. I wouldn't necessarily call Jay a "bully." I think he, along with many boys and girls (and men and women), unfortunately have no idea how to communicate their true feelings sometimes. And I can see how that has something to do with fear and I'm sure we've all been there.

Anyway, I am certain that if we could all grasp how wide and long and high and deep the Father's love is for us, internal and global wars would cease. And there you have it: world peace!

A found picture of me in my soccer jersey and shorts at the age of nine inspired that post. I remember finding it and being excited to show Mike. I told him that it was this year in my life that I really started hating my thighs and other things about myself. We both cried because they were good legs. I stood confident, with one hand on my hip and the other holding a soccer ball. Mike couldn't talk but his look said it all: *You were beautiful then and you are beautiful now!*

He loved that picture and he loved me for me. He mirrored God's love by loving me just the way I was, unconditionally.

Oh, this journey of love! This tremendous, wonderful, sometimes painful journey of love. My twenty-seven-plus years with Mike taught me so much about it, like any enduring relationship does. Those last few years though, we were immersed in a love that pushed through the limits we had previously placed on it. A love that we might not have ever experienced had we not been tossed into the turbulent world of ALS.

The next post is the last one I wrote before Mike passed away. I'll let the love speak for itself…

Typical Mike - Dec 28, 2014

It's really late and I should be sleeping. But instead, I lie here in bed listening to one of my favourite Christmas songs and the sound of my beloved Michael breathing. My heart is absolutely full and my cheeks are soaking wet and I wonder how I will ever explain what's going on inside of me. In four minutes, it will be December 27, 2014, and I am grateful beyond words for another night with Mike and the sound of his breath as he peacefully sleeps. Every night I wonder if tonight will be the last time we say goodbye.

It's been a unique Christmas. Some things are the

same, but some are very different. Mike says this will most likely be our last Christmas together here on earth, so we are savouring every moment.

We are having a wonderful time with family, but our times alone are extraordinary. The tender moments between sessions of suctioning, uncontrollable coughing and bowel care are sweet. It's like there's a glow. Maybe it's all the Christmas lights I put up this year because Mike loves Christmas lights, but it's a special glow, like angels are among us. It's been a time of last words, and every day I wonder why I'm so lucky to be able to say goodbye like this. Nothing will go unsaid.

I tell Mike every day that I love him, and he gives me the look *I love you, too*. A while ago when I told Mike "I love you," he wanted the alphabet board. I picked it up and held it right in front of him like I'd done a hundred times before.

I started, "A? E? I?"

He raised his eyebrow slightly at "I."

"Is it the letter 'I' or is 'I' the word?" I inquired. Yes, "I" was the word.

Then I moved on. "A, E, I?" It's "I" again. I asked if it's the letter "I" and got a slight nod no. "J, K, L?" It's "L." I questioned Mike if it's "love." He raised his brows.

"You love me back?" I asked. He smiled and kept going.

"I love you more than ever," he spelled. With a lump in my throat, I told him I loved him more than ever, too.

When we moved out of our little three-storey house and into my sister Elanna and her husband Peter's ground-level basement suite two and a half years ago when we could no longer manage the stairs, I found some old home movies we had never converted to DVD. I put the little tapes in a box with the intention of having them switched to discs, but I forgot.

A couple of months ago, they came to my mind and I finally took them in to be transferred. The DVDs were ready just before Christmas, so I wrapped them up and put them under the tree for Mike. Turns out, it was the best present I could have received. After Christmas dinner, we all gathered around the TV and watched one of the discs. I randomly chose one marked "new house," not knowing what we'd find. It was perfect! Mike was behind the camera most of the time. It started at our old townhouse on 236 Street with our three children and some of their friends in the backyard. Mike also showed the empty rooms and packed boxes, as we were in the middle of a move.

Then Mike was at the river filming the kids and friends floating on rafts and then swimming in the swimming hole called Davison's Pool. Suddenly, at one point, there was Mike, lying on an air mattress on the rock next to the water, tanning in the sun. A random woman came up to him and offered to put lotion on his back.

All smiles and flirty, Mike was like, "Sure, what's your name?"

She replied, "Anything you want it to be," and proceeded to rub him down with lotion.

We were killing ourselves laughing. This skit and other antics is typical Mike Sands. There was also some footage of Mike and our oldest daughter Erin on a trip to Toronto that summer. His mum and dad were there, along with his siblings and some nieces and nephews. It was really cool. The video ended in our new backyard with little Michaela and Luke, Elanna and Peter's two children, playing fetch with our dear departed dog, Isla. It was so special.

In one scene at the townhouse, we were loading up a truck and moving to our new house (the little three-story house) on Mountainview Crescent. Our youngest daughter Madison sat in a chair in the back of the truck. I had the camera in the passenger's seat and our son, Nathan, was in the middle. Mike climbed into the driver's seat, started the engine and began singing, "And they loaded up the truck and they moved to Beverly ... Hills that is, swimmin' pools, movie stars..."

Again, typical Mike ... the wisecracks about Granny in the back, the jokes, the laughs—that was Mike! His silliness ten years ago and the laughs they produced this Christmas Day was the greatest gift he could have given me and all of us. And the ear-to-ear grin on his face while he watched was priceless.

When I put Mike to bed that night, I couldn't contain the tears, which isn't that unusual these days. I apologized for not appreciating him more: his silliness, his jokes, his love for making me and others laugh.

To be honest, sometimes his almost constant joking around got on my nerves. In that moment, I could only remember how unkind I was to him sometimes and how loving he was to me. I hugged him and cried and said I was sorry.

Then Mike wanted to say something. It took a while with the alphabet board, but this is what he said, "In all the years we've been together, you've never judged me for the countless mistakes I made."

I replied, "What mistakes?"

He continued, "See, you've forgotten them already. Heaven is about love and forgiveness—you are already there." He went on to say, "You are the perfect girl for me … God gave me the perfect wife."

Mike would often tell me that he was so lucky to marry the girl of his dreams and how I was his "sweetheart." But tonight I didn't feel like a "sweetheart." I felt like a failure. I wanted to go back in time and show him more love and truly embrace the joy he brought into our lives.

I really don't recall Mike making many mistakes and he apparently has forgotten mine—even though we both made many, of course. I guess that's what love and forgiveness is all about. It's about forgetting, or at least not counting the other's faults. Mike has spelled out to me a few times, "Heaven is about love and forgiveness."

Hebrews 8:12 says, "For I will be merciful toward their iniquities, and I will remember their sins no more." (ESV)

To forgive and forget is to love with the love of Christ.

I'm finishing this post here in my bed next to Mike. It's weird because in three minutes it will be December 28th, exactly twenty-four hours and one minute after I started writing this post. Mike is fast asleep beside me and my ears are attentive to his every breath. His breathing is like beautiful music to me and I'm so thankful for twenty-four hours and one minute more with my beloved Mike.

Love keeps no record of wrongs! Easier said than done sometimes, I know, but what a remarkable place to be when you really don't recall the other's mistakes. Mike and I came to a place where love and forgiveness was exactly the same, and forgetting was part of the package. I remember thinking later that if I really thought hard, I could dredge up lots of things. But why bother? The layers of love became layers of cement over the years—a freshly-paved road. All the potholes were filled and the bumps smoothed over. If I took a jackhammer, I could have dug up something (and so could he), but why disrupt the Master's handiwork—a road paved with His phenomenal grace.

Love is also patient, and communication with the alphabet board, and many other aspects of ALS, definitely taught us something about patience. Mike had a perfectly good communication device for quite some time, but it required movement of his head. A little camera on the laptop picked up the reflection from a silver sticker we stuck on the end of his nose. The device was called Head Mouse. He moved the little shiny dot around the on-screen keyboard to type words. Then he'd hover it over a "speak" key to vocalize them.

He lost the ability to move his head when the last remaining muscles in his body—his neck muscles—quit. That was it. He had a few appointments with someone who taught him how to use a device called Eye Gaze. Obstacles in that process kept him from really learning it, so for the few months leading up to his death, it was the alphabet board for us.

It sure was a long and tiresome way to communicate. But just like all the challenges of this illness, we persevered together and we worked together. We got frustrated together and trusted God together. We laughed and cried together and surrendered together. We met God on higher planes together and in the depths of despair. And that is where we got to know Him better and experienced His pure and perfect love like never before.

"Love is patient, love is kind. It does not envy, it does not boast, it is not proud. It does not dishonour others, it is not self-seeking, it is not easily angered, it keeps no record of wrongs. Love does not delight in evil but rejoices with the truth. It always protects, always trusts, always hopes, always perseveres. Love never fails."
I Corinthians 13: 4-8 (NIV)

Mike passed away eight days after I wrote "Typical Mike."

Three months later my book *Hold On, Let Go* launched, and shortly after that I had a number of speaking engagements.

One of them was for a Christian Women's event with the theme: "Be Brave."

I called my speech "Worrier to Warrior" and read a few stories from my book to help my audience get a glimpse of the kind of guy Mike was—how inspiring and brave he was. And then I went on with something like this…

After contemplating "courage" and praying for courage and praying about what it is to be brave, I came to this conclusion. At first, I thought that being brave meant something different for each of us. For example, for Mike, who was a really private person, sharing his journey with ALS to the world through my blog was brave and so was being grateful and content in the face of death. For me today, being brave is getting up here and speaking to all of you … with a big lump in my throat. And maybe for some of you, being brave is confronting someone who has hurt you, or maybe it's simply saying, "I Love You," OR "Please forgive me," OR "I need help." But it's not different for all of us. Being brave is the same for each one of us. We are all courageous by being vulnerable.

In my book I compare myself to my friend Carol and refer to her as a "window" and myself as a "wall." I tell how her transparency drew me in all those years ago. How her gutsy way of letting her true colours show was beauty to me. I did everything I could to cover up my flaws and imperfections. She didn't, and I found that refreshing. There was a joy in her vulnerability. I write how she has inspired me to be more window, less wall.

Being vulnerable can lead to rejection but way more often it ties us together. We sometimes think being brave means we have to be something we aren't - to armour up or wear a cape, like Wonder Woman - but it's the opposite. It's about being our imperfect selves, it's about sharing from the heart, relating and connecting and understanding.

While preparing this speech, I was excited to come across Brené Brown's TED talk, The Power of Vulnerability, which validated my thoughts and ideas about the subject. She explains, "The original definition of 'courage' is from the Latin word 'cor,' meaning 'heart.' The original definition was to tell the story of who you are with your whole heart... this myth that vulnerability is weakness, keeps us afraid when the truth is vulnerability is our greatest measure of courage."

To go from worrier to warrior, I've learned that you have to do the opposite of what the world might think. You have to take down the walls you've constructed, get rid of the capes and the drapes, and let the bright light shine through your window. Be brave by being vulnerably beautiful you!

I've given this speech on several occasions, changing parts of it here and there each time. I feel like it's two steps forward and one step back sometimes, and sometimes the other way around when it comes to being vulnerable. I struggle with being completely real. I hold things back in fear. This window is still under construction. But as long as God calls me to tell my story, I will share from my heart as authentically as I can, trusting Him. That's what it's really about—trusting Him.

I have long learned that He is perfectly trustworthy even though it seems I need Him to keep reminding me. I know for sure that His ways are higher than mine. His plans are perfect, yet still I vie for the control sometimes. So here I am, still learning to let go and still learning by His grace how to wrap my little brain around the vastness of His love.

This next story is way out of chronological order, but it fits nicely right here...

Love Is In the Air - Feb 12, 2016

I begin this fresh blog post with the topic of "love" on my mind. Not only is Valentine's Day almost here, but I've fallen hard for a special someone. So, I've got "love" as a starting point and will let my fingers do their thing on my laptop keyboard. It feels good to start something new.

I've been working on a speech I'm giving called Worrier to Warrior – finding hope, joy and courage after a terminal diagnosis.

I'm afraid that my title might give the wrong impression. It might make people think I have it all figured out like I'm some kind of "Wonder Woman." And when they find out the opposite is true, they might boo. Seriously though, it is the opposite of a "Wonder Woman" story and more of a "living hopefully, joyfully and courageously with a big lump in my throat" story. A "totally relying on God, trusting in Him, falling down and getting back up again, I could never do this on my own" story. It's an "expose your soul, be completely vulnerable, just let go, He's got you, so be brave" story.

All good titles, and now I'm a little disappointed about the one I chose. Anyway, back to my blog post. Turning to a new page and writing about something else is refreshing, so here goes...

I start my love story at my lovely round glass table by my big living room window with the beautiful scenery in my peripheral view. Glen is on my lap. I don't think I've said much about Glen in my blogging, but if you are a Facebook friend, you've seen a picture or a few of him. Glen is Madison's dog. When we talked about moving from my sister's house, Madison told me she really wanted to get a dog. Even though she adored the couple of pound dogs she has had in the past, she said this time she was going to get a dog of her favourite breed, a pug.

She found him online in Oregon and the breeder thankfully met her at the US/Canada border. He was eight weeks old and fit in one hand, the cutest thing you'd ever seen—all those wonderful wrinkles, those big bulging eyes and that cinnamon bun swirl of a tail that sits on the top of his back end. He's getting bigger and isn't quite fitting on my lap the way he did, but he makes it work as best he can with his limbs and head spilling over.

When Madison told me about getting Glen, I was opposed to the idea. I thought about my new floors, the fur, the dirt, the puppy accidents and the chewed up stuff. I definitely expressed my concern, but there is something else I was concerned about that I didn't mention: the love.

I thought about the love I'd feel for this little one, and then one day I'd have to say goodbye. Like I have done before with pets, including our dog Isla who I watched take her last breath. And, of course, the same with Mike. Deep down, I was terrified to love this little guy, but I used the excuse of fur and dirt and puppy pee.

I could see that Madison had already fallen for him, so I had no choice but to open the door … and down came the wall when this little fur ball walked in.

I guess I had started constructing a wall to keep out the love because what I've learned over the years, especially the last couple, is that love can really hurt sometimes. And what do we do to prevent hurting? We put up walls, we close doors, we try to keep the hurt out. I guess I thought I'd just never let myself love again, whether it be another puppy, another man, or new friend. But to be courageous, you have to be vulnerable and if I want to stay true to my "vulnerability equals bravery" theory that I preach in my speech, I have to open the door. It's tough, but love conquers all, right? Shouldn't love overshadow fear? My head says yes, but my heart still says ouch a little. Slowly, we're getting there.

So far, Glen hasn't brought any hurting into the equations, only joy and healing. Regardless of the potential pain and the lump in my throat and the dirty floors, I have fallen in love with the little guy. And I shall continue to conquer my fears by living hopefully, joyfully and courageously by being vulnerable and trusting God with all my heart.

"To love at all is to be vulnerable. Love anything and your heart will be wrung and possibly broken. If you want to make sure of keeping it intact you must give it to no one, not even an animal. Wrap it carefully round with hobbies and little luxuries; avoid all entanglements. Lock it up safe in the casket or coffin of your selfishness. But in that casket, safe, dark, motionless, airless, it will change. It will not be broken; it will become unbreakable, impenetrable, irredeemable. To love is to be vulnerable."

C.S. Lewis

Shortly after I wrote "Love is in the Air," I realized I was being prepared for something bigger. Could I be vulnerable enough to open my heart to the love of another man, or keep it closed and safe? But before that, there was a plethora of healing to be done in me, so on with the comforting power of grief.

Family photo,
June 2008
Nathan's graduation

Family photo (post ALS diagnosis), June 2012 - Madison's graduation

CHAPTER 2
High Hopes and Anchor Ropes

"We have this hope as an anchor for the soul, firm and secure."
Hebrews 6:19 (NIV)

Mike wasn't a hugger. He didn't like hugging; it made him uncomfortable. It was kind of foreign to him when we first met, but just the opposite for me and my family. If someone went in for a hug, he'd step back and extend a hand for a shake instead. Often, I'd grab him and take his arms and wrap them around me, and I'd wrap mine around him. I'd whisper, "Tighter."

Over time, Mike came to understand I needed more affection than he did, although I sometimes still had to use the above method to remind him. He was very affectionate with our children when they were small and held them a lot. He hugged them and kissed their heads. I can still see him bouncing them around and kissing their heads. When Mike went to visit his family in Ontario (times I didn't go with him), I'd call and ask if he'd hugged his mum yet. I'd tell him to be sure to give her a hug when he left.

It wasn't long after Mike's ALS diagnosis that he lost the use of his arms. I still try to remember when he last hugged me for real, when he could still squeeze tight. I can't remember.

When he was unable to stand on his own, I stood him up to stretch him out after sitting for a while. I leaned his body up against mine and took his limp arms and put them around me, holding them there with one hand and hugging him with the other. He rested his head on my shoulder. When we made love, I took his hand and placed it on my thigh or elsewhere, and often wondered when the last time was that he reached out on his own. Or, when did we last press our palms together and interlock fingers. I couldn't remember.

I started a new journal two days before Mike's diagnosis. I journaled almost every day for about eight months until I started my ALS With Courage blog. Two days after Mike's diagnosis, I wrote the following:

Journal entry from March 9, 2011

We woke up early and just held each other. Then I prayed. Mike shared that this ALS diagnosis is a very humbling experience. We talked about the fragility of life and how much our bodies are like tents; it's the spirit inside of course that counts and lives when tents are wrecked.

We read our daily Oswald Chambers reading. He says, "All that is required is to live a natural life of absolute dependence on Jesus Christ. Never try to live your life with God in any other way than His way. And His way means absolute devotion to Him. Showing no concern for the uncertainties that lie ahead is the secret of walking with Jesus."

Then we read from the Book of John. John 6:63a (NIV) says, "The Spirit gives life, the flesh counts for nothing." How appropriate! Mike and I both agreed how comforting God's Word is. We talked some more and held each other's hand tightly. I told him he was the love of my life … he told me I was his.

My mom and dad, and Nathan, Elanna and Carol came for tea. We had lots of laughs. Mike went for lunch with the kids. Later when we were alone, Mike said to me with big tears in his eyes, "We have such amazing kids." I replied, "I know." We hugged. Elanna told me last night that we had done such a great job with our children. I responded, "With lots of help from the Lord."

When I mentioned certain friends and family that we have yet to tell this news, Mike started to cry. We hugged some more. We had a few teary hugs. It's the first time Mike has ever cried on my shoulder. I felt good to be able to be strong for him. By God's grace, I am strong for him.

Tonight we read from 1 Peter 4:1-2 (NIV) which says, "Therefore, since Christ suffered in His body, arm yourselves also with the same attitude, because whoever suffers in his body is done with sin. As a result, they do not live the rest of their earthly lives for evil human desires, but rather for the will of God." Verse 19 says, "So then, those who suffer according to God's will should commit themselves to their faithful Creator and continue to do good."

One last thought. It's going to be a grieving process. I've experienced it before, but not this devastating, of course. I've had hopes and dreams about other things that have completely fallen apart. But God is so good and quickly gave me new hopes and dreams for those other things and He will do the same for me and Mike.

~

Forever You'll Stay in My Heart - Jan 20, 2015

Our goal as a family was to honour Mike and to bless everyone who came to his memorial service with glimpses of his life, but the blessings fell heavy on us. For me, it was like a downpour of love and support. I had no idea how blessed I was going to be. Regarding the hundreds of hugs I received, I thought Mike would be so happy because he hadn't been able to hug me in a very long time. It was like hug therapy.

Pastor Art started Mike's service with some exceptionally wonderful words. I can't remember them exactly, but everything he said meant so much to me and honoured Mike perfectly. He thoughtfully spoke with such eloquence. One thing Pastor Art explained during his beautiful tribute was, "Mike didn't necessarily say 'I love you;' he showed it."

Mike wasn't great at expressing with words how he felt, but he certainly tried to let his actions speak louder than words. His motto was "Talk is cheap" and "Walk the walk."

A number of months ago, feeling the need to say "I love you" to our children, Mike dictated a message to me to relay to them. It included a quote from one of our favourite songs, "You Are the Sunshine of My Life" by Stevie Wonder. It was one of the songs we used for Mike's slideshow.

Because the memorial service fell on Mike's birthday (January 16) and because Mike had not really eaten anything by mouth for over a year and a half before he passed, I asked Pastor Brad, who spoke next, to please speak about the banquet table in heaven.

In September of 2013, I wrote a blog post called "Heaven Scent" about Mike's journey of letting go of food. I called it what I did because after our many summer evening walks, Mike and I thought that heaven could very well smell like the incredible scent of BBQ. The following is some of that post:

A few months ago, when Mike's food selection was becoming more and more limited and we were both becoming more and more disappointed, I would visualize a banquet table laid out for him in heaven. A table covered with the most mouth-watering dishes imaginable. If we saw a big, fat, juicy hamburger advertised on TV, I'd tell him that it was going to be at his "big feast."

It was very appropriate that a sermon preached this summer by Brad was on this very subject. The sermon topic was on hospitality, but Brad spoke about the banquet table in heaven. I loved hearing him describe the dinner, or "party" as he put it. It helped with my vision of Mike's feast ... a meal fit for a king! In the presence of the King of Kings!

Brad quoted Isaiah 25:6 (NIV) which says, "The Lord Almighty will prepare a feast of rich food for all peoples, a banquet of aged wine—the best of meats and the finest of wines." I say, "Cheers, Mike!"

Pastor Trevor concluded the service and quoted one of Erin's Facebook posts: "I know that today you are running miles and miles with that big smile on your face. One day we will run together again. Your chains are gone, you've been set free!"

I had asked Trevor to please say something about Mike leaving his earthly body behind and receiving a new, perfect one in heaven. No more illness, no more ALS! Trevor could not have done a better job portraying Mike's new life in God's domain—running free with no more chains!

A CELEBRATION OF LIFE

MICHAEL DAVID SANDS

January 16, 1962 ~ January 5, 2015

When we were all saying goodbye to my mom before she died, I asked her to please give Mike a big hug from us in heaven. I told her that when they embraced, it wouldn't be one of his lame hugs or one of his limp ALS hugs. It would be an awesome one—a really strong and long one.

I've got grief for my loss and then I've got all this grief for theirs, for others who loved him with all their hearts, especially our kids. It's intense sometimes, mostly on occasions to celebrate or to commiserate. Their dad isn't there.

Mike worked a lot, and even though he did his best to be at all their games and other events, he just wasn't around as much as I'm sure they wished he was, emotionally perhaps, especially during those tough teenage years. He and I just did what we thought was best. Mike worked more and I worked less. Economically, it made the best sense and I was thrilled to be home after school when the kids walked through the door. It was one of the greatest blessings of my life, thanks to Mike and how he sacrificed.

Here is one reason why ALS was a gift: I've said it before and I'll say it again, it gave us time. For three years and ten months, our children could see their dad whenever they wanted. They spent a lot of time sharing fond memories. They shared many laughs, some tears, and even a few hugs.

Regrets concerning some of the decisions we made around how to raise our children still linger. Same with the disappointment I feel for them—for the hole in their hearts that will remain until they meet their dad again. Perhaps I still grieve some of the dashed hopes and dreams and definitely the feeling of Mike's hand pressed against mine and his head on my shoulder.

The "nerd" with his girls on their last Halloween together. They trick-or-treated every year together. The girls continue the tradition.

Good Grief - Jan 27, 2015

How can "good" and "grief" go together? Aren't they opposites? "Good" is good and "grief" is bad … right?

When I hear the expression "Good grief," I think of Charlie Brown, who is famous for it. I love Charlie Brown. Poor little guy, nothing ever seems to go his way. We are big fans of him, Snoopy and the Peanuts gang. As a family, we have two Charlie Brown specials that we like to watch in particular: the Halloween special, *It's the Great Pumpkin, Charlie Brown* and the Christmas special, *A Charlie Brown Christmas.*

The kids know exactly where I start to tear up in *A Charlie Brown Christmas*, and they give me the look like, are you going to cry again? Linus' explanation of what Christmas is all about gets me every time, along with the scene where the Peanuts gang transforms Charlie Brown's sad little Christmas tree into a spectacular display of ornaments and lights.

What we like best about *It's the Great Pumpkin, Charlie Brown* is the Peanuts gang comparing what they get after trick or treating at each house. One says, "I got a chocolate bar." Another, "I got a pack of gum." And another, "I got a quarter." Charlie Brown exclaims, "I got a rock!" He gets a rock every time.

Anyway, back to good grief. I've been learning how grieving is good and how my mourning involves a little rock collecting of its own. One day last week, I woke up with rocks on the brain, not to be confused with "rocks for brains." Rocks were simply on my mind. All of a sudden, I needed rocks. With way more important things to do, I was off to the river.

Pastor Art gave me some wise advice a few days after Mike passed away. He reminded me of Matthew 5:4 which says, "Blessed are those who mourn, for they will be comforted." (NIV) He said that sometimes we busy ourselves and avoid grieving, but only when we grieve do we fully experience God's comfort.

Curious about "mourning," I did a little research on the internet and found that grief is the beginning of mourning. Grief is what you feel or think when someone dies, or when you lose someone or something (including divorce, illness, injury, loss of a job, a beloved pet, treasured possessions, and so on). Mourning is how you let it out in outward expression, actions and reactions. There are five stages of grief: denial, anger, bargaining, depression and acceptance. I think I'm still in the shock/numb stage—numb is normal, as well as shock, sadness, guilt, and anger.

I told Pastor Art that I wasn't going to try to be happy and I wasn't going to try to be sad. I was just going to "be" and see where that took me. I wanted to be available to God and whatever He had planned for me in the "mourning." I'm trying to heed Pastor Art's advice to not busy myself and avoid grieving. I'll admit I'm not necessarily embracing it, but I have started collecting rocks.

I don't think I've fully grieved the loss of pre-ALS Mike. The man who took care of me, who held me and kissed me and enveloped me with his strong arms and legs in our warm bed. He was like my cocoon and I, his butterfly.

The losses came fast and furious and I could barely keep up. Some things I'm over, some I'm not. I've got a lot of catching up to do. But now I can truly grieve, and even though I'm a little scared of what that's going to look like, I invite the comfort of the Lord to envelop me … to be my cocoon and I, His butterfly.

That's what it really feels like - being enveloped by the strong embrace of God's love and grace. It's caterpillar-to-butterfly transforming. Even though that journal I kept after Mike's diagnosis is filled with accounts of uncontrollable tears, overwhelming sadness and fear, it's also filled with excellent memories and encouragement from God's Word. It's filled with joy, peace and new perspective. The greater the grief and pain, the sweeter God's embrace. That's what I've learned along the way.

I've also learned some things about the extraordinary power of hope, including this: without it, you have nothing!

Hope Goes a Long Way - Feb 5, 2015

I'll never forget that Christmas morning smile. When I woke up and looked at Mike, he was as bright as the Christmas lights. My first thought was, *He's happy to be here for Christmas.*

Mike wanted to say something to me right away, so I got the alphabet. "I would have said Merry Christmas at 5:55, but I can't talk," he spelled. He had to go pee early in the morning and I mentioned the time … 5:55.

The sadness is starting to sink in. I'm past the shocked/numb stage that I talked about in my last post, although I'm still a little shocked (and still collecting rocks).

I'd give anything to go back to Christmas morning, just to get a glimpse of his smile one more time. It's like I didn't see it coming, but everything leading up to Mike's passing was a clue it was near. I feel kind of dumb now, but I think God was preparing me and protecting me at the same time.

The following is a quote from my November 29 post, "Trooper."

After Mike was all tucked in, I said, "Let's pray." I stood beside his bed and started to speak. I opened my mouth and, without thinking, the words spilled out; the Spirit moved in a mighty way. I could barely keep up with the words; it was like a river of words flowed from my mouth and a river of tears flowed down my face. I ended the prayer by saying, "Lord, whether we have a really short time left together, or if we have more time than we think, please prepare us to part."

I asked God to prepare us to part a few times. Looking back, it's obvious He had been preparing us for a while. Even though it was inevitable, it still didn't feel like it was actually going to happen. When it did, I was just so surprised. You can be somewhat ready to die, but very conditioned to live and hopeful to the very last minute. I was hopeful to the end that a miracle would happen, that the love of my life would be lifted right off death's doorstep. Hope goes a long way and I think it's one way God protects us.

Mike was ready to let go for quite a while before he finally did. I think he stuck around for me and the kids and the rest of the family, but he had heaven on his mind for a long time. The following journal entry speaks of his readiness.

Journal entry from November 16, 2014

Tonight, after a long session of suctioning in the bathroom (Mike was on his commode), while down on my knees cleaning up things, Mike and I caught each other's eyes and exchanged a long smile. Then he motioned for the alphabet. With the same smile, he spelled out, "I can't wait to see you in heaven." When he got to the word "you," I knew what he was going to say and was overcome with emotion. Able to hold it in, I only started crying at the word "heaven."

~

I told Mike that I'd meet him for a picnic when I got there, and whispered the same thing in his ear a few minutes before he died.

Mike has been taken off death's doorstep all right and is fully alive on the other side. I can only wonder what he's been up to. At some point, he'll size up a nice patch of grass by a quiet stream for a very special picnic reunion. I don't know if things work like that in heaven, but I can dream.

I'm sure we've all heard the words, "Don't get your hopes up." The higher the hopes, the greater the devastation when they come crashing down, I guess. But I have no regrets about remaining hopeful to the very end. The night before Mike passed away, I honestly thought we were going home the next day. Our forty-eight-hour hospital stay was just enough to get some much needed deep suctioning and some oxygen to take with us, and we'd be on our way. Tests showed a collapsed lung, but that was nothing for him.

What was I thinking? I guess I just thought my Superman, this man of steel, was unbeatable. His spirit, yes! His body, not so much. My hope, though, kept me going. It kept my head up. It kept me joyful. It kept my soul anchored to the One I know. The One who is bigger than us, bigger than ALS. The One who holds the perfect plan in His hand. Definitely not my plan, far from my plan, but this is where letting go and where trust comes in.

Definitions for hope include words like anticipation, optimism, wishing, desiring, believing something will happen, or that something is possible. Researching the biblical usage of hope, I find words like trust, certainty, confident expectation, look for, wait for, endure, to expect something good in the future. Biblical hope isn't wishful thinking; it is believing in God's promises. It is about trusting in Him. Hope is tied to faith; the two are actually joined at the hip. "Now faith is confidence in what we hope for and assurance about what we do not see." Hebrews 11:1 (NIV)

Hope leads to faith and love. Colossians 1:4-5 (NLT) says, "For we have heard of your faith in Christ Jesus and your love for all of God's people, which come from your confident hope of what God has reserved for you in heaven. You have had this expectation ever since you first heard the truth of the Good News."

There was, of course, a lot of sorrow in our ALS experience, up to and beyond death, but there was also a steadfast joy and peace. Just like the faith/hope partnership, hope, joy and peace are also a team. Romans 15:13 (NIV) says, "May the God of hope fill you with all joy and peace as you trust in him, so that you may overflow with hope by the power of the Holy Spirit." A few chapters back, there's this: "Be joyful in hope, patient in affliction, faithful in prayer." The Passion Translation says it like this: "Let this hope burst forth within you, releasing a continual joy. Don't give up in a time of trouble, but commune with God at all times."

Our "God of hope" did not promise a cure on this earth for our illnesses, or escape from disaster, even death. Instead He states, "In this world you will have trouble. But take heart! I have overcome the world." John 16:33 (NIV) He also said, "For I know the plans I have for you. Plans to prosper you and not to harm you, plans to give you hope and a future." Jeremiah 29:11 (NIV)

"When you go through deep waters, I will be with you. When you go through rivers of difficulty, you will not drown."
Isaiah 43:2 (NLT)

"I am the resurrection and the life. Anyone who believes in me will live, even after dying."
John 11:25 (NLT)

"I am leaving you with a gift—peace of mind and heart. And the peace I give is a gift the world cannot give. So don't be troubled or afraid. Remember what I told you: I am going away, but I will come back to you again..."
John 14:27–28 (NLT)

As a child of the God of Hope, I've inherited this glorious characteristic of hope, and trust it will remain through thick and thin. So even when my husband is taking his last breath, there's hope, because it's just in me. Even though God didn't provide the miracle I desired of healing or a cure, He provided a miracle of redemption and my beloved had long put his hope in higher things. In heavenly things. In Jesus.

I say, "Get your hopes up!" Mike's death brought me intense disappointment, yes, and surpassed sorrow for sure. But it brought him new life, freedom and complete healing. It brought him face to face with his Redeemer and best Friend, Jesus. Mike's hope never failed him. Mine hasn't failed either. My soul—anchored to the One above everything else—remained and remains full of hope.

Even though I still hope for a cure for ALS and healing for others' illnesses and many things, my hope is so much more than an expectation in something; it's a confident expectation and assured certainty in Someone.

Take Courage, I Am Here! - Feb 27, 2015

I don't like going to bed. When I'm totally exhausted it's okay, but I avoid going because it's the biggest reminder that Mike's not here. I used to love going to bed and listening to music with Mike, watching him drift off to sleep. Sometimes, after I put him down and went and got ready myself, he was already asleep when I climbed in. Sometimes I wrote, sometimes I read, sometimes I curled up as close to him as I possibly could and sometimes I just stared at him until the weight of my eyelids took over. I never liked giving in to the sleep that always beckoned me because then I had to say goodbye to another day with my beloved Mike. And I knew that our days were drawing to an end.

For the first few weeks after Mike passed, I stayed up until about two o'clock in the morning most of the time. I only went to bed when I knew I was going to crash the second I laid down my head. I've slowly been able to turn in a little earlier, like midnight or 1:00 a.m., usually reading or something. Tonight, I'm writing this blog post and listening to music (right now I'm listening to one of our favourite songs, "Oceans," by Hillsong United). I'm still struggling to fully surrender to the mourning. I keep wondering what will happen in six months or twelve months. Will it hit me then? Will I drown then?

I really feel if I step out into this huge ocean of mourning, I will drown … so I just sit in the boat and patiently wait for the waves to subside. Even if the waves subside, I'll probably stay put because I'm afraid. I'm afraid if I step out, I'll sink; I'll drown. This ocean of mourning is huge and from the middle of it, the shore is nowhere to be found.

The above is how I feel, but below is what I know: Matthew 14:22-33 (NLT) says, "Meanwhile, the disciples were in trouble far away from land, for a strong wind had risen, and they were fighting heavy waves. About three o'clock in the morning, Jesus came toward them, walking on the water. When the disciples saw Him walking on the water, they were terrified. In their fear, they cried out, 'It's a ghost!' But Jesus spoke to them at once. 'Don't be afraid,' He said. 'Take courage. I am here!' Then Peter called to Him, 'Lord, if it's really You, tell me to come to You, walking on the water.' 'Yes, come,' Jesus said. So Peter went over the side of the boat and walked on the water toward Jesus. But when he saw the strong wind and the waves, he was terrified and began to sink. 'Save me, Lord!' he shouted. Jesus immediately reached out and grabbed him. 'You have so little faith,' Jesus said. 'Why did you doubt me?' When they climbed back into the boat, the wind stopped. Then the disciples worshiped him. 'You really are the Son of God!' they exclaimed."

At 2:00 a.m., alone in my bed, Jesus says, "Take courage, I am here!" His eyes are on me like mine were on Mike, except His eyelids never get tired. And eventually when I step out of this boat, if I should sink, I know He'll be there to catch me.

P.S. My dad and Nathan are back from their trip to Malawi, where two wells were drilled a few weeks ago through our family's society, Project Wellness. One of the wells is the memorial well that was drilled in Mike's name. Thank you to everyone who contributed to this very precious gift that will serve many people in a very special African village. Access to clean water is a matter of life and death ... thanks for your gift of life! My dad chose the Bible verse from Matthew 25:23 and inscribed it on Mike's well: "Well done, good and faithful servant."

Nathan at Mike's memorial well in Malawi, Africa.

I've referred to hope as a rope before, like a lifeline to the Lord and this anchor I talk about. But, over the years, on a few occasions, my hope has definitely dangled by a thread. He is so faithful, though. His unfailing love and comfort renews hope!

"I cried out, 'I am slipping!' but Your unfailing love, O Lord, supported me. When doubts filled my mind, Your comfort gave me renewed hope and cheer."
Psalm 94:18-19 (NLT)

CHAPTER 3
It's OK. Judge my Book by its Cover

"The faithful love of the Lord never ends! His mercies never cease.
Great is His faithfulness; His mercies begin afresh each morning."
Lamentations 3:22-23 (NLT)

My goal when I wrote Hold On, Let Go was to have it written before Mike passed away. Quite the incentive, hey? Looking back, I almost laugh. I was so diligent. I was going to school part-time, teaching fitness classes a few hours a week, blogging occasionally, writing a book, and mostly taking care of Mike.

When Mike's caregivers were there, I'd hide away in Peter's home office and write. I wrote at night when Mike was sleeping, during Judge Judy, Seinfeld reruns and NHL hockey games. While Mike sat on his commode in the washroom, I sometimes sat there too, on the lid of the toilet seat, running sentences and paragraphs by him. I kept my laptop almost as close as I kept the suction machine. I couldn't let myself get distracted by Facebook or anything, like I do now. I had to stay focused. I was on a mission. Sometimes it felt a little lonely, often overwhelming. Looking back and remembering myself immersed in writing and caring for Mike, God was so present. At the time, I didn't always feel it or take notice, but now when

I close my eyes, I see God's hands on my hands directing the flow of my laptop keyboard and the gentle care of my darling Mike.

The day Mike passed away was the day my final typesetting edits were due. I've mentioned before that the editing process is huge. There are different stages; it's long and tiresome. I had recruited my friend Donna to proof it in that final stage and my sister and mom (who had helped all along). I ran home from the hospital to email my publisher with the final edits shortly before Mike died. I compiled the corrections during those couple of days at the hospital by Mike's side. Elanna stayed with Mike so I knew he was in good hands, but had I known that it was his last day with us, of course I never would have left him.

Sending off those last edits and saying goodbye to Mike on the same day now seems crazy. I recently explained to a friend who was in the final stage of editing, how there is this grieving effect when you let go of it. You send it off, wondering if it's okay, if it's good enough; wondering if you shared enough, or too much. Your soul is now done pouring itself out. Words cease. Your mind wraps itself around letting go, around giving your story away. And then you wait, soon to be exposed to the whole world. And you don't know how not to dedicate every waking thought to writing that book.

I Hope You'll Judge My Book By Its Cover - Feb 15, 2015

Sometimes, all of a sudden I think, "Oh, yeah, he's not there," and my stomach burns; my heart aches. Mike has always been there. I met him when I was eighteen, married him when I was nineteen, and for almost twenty-seven years he was there. Now, he's gone. I'm totally lost without him. When he left, a part of me left too and the rest of me is just kind of wandering around.

I never feel alone though. God is very close; He is so merciful. It's the first thing I said after Mike passed. I told Elanna, "God is so merciful." She agreed. The Bible tells us that God's mercies are new every morning. I'm convinced they are new every minute. During my "mourning" His mercy carries me.

Merriam-Webster defines mercy like this: "A blessing that is an act of divine favour or compassion, kindness or help to people who are in a very bad or desperate situation."

God is rich in mercy and He is love and this is how I go on.

On Friday, I went to a workshop downtown. It was a public speaking workshop for authors of Influence Publishing. I knew it wasn't going to be easy, but I signed up anyway (I need all the help I can get when it comes to public speaking). Although it was exhausting, I'm really glad I went. I wholeheartedly engaged with the other authors and feel like I made some new friends; however, I only halfheartedly participated in the various exercises. I had to be reserved; I could only give so much.

The instructions of one exercise were to state your name, the name of your book and to give a very short description, all in thirty seconds. This is what I said: "It's a 'stay positive in difficult times story' about my husband, Michael Sands, who was diagnosed with ALS in March of 2011, and our journey with terminal illness. It's about giving thanks in every circumstance, having faith, being hopeful and, bottom line, it's about love! My book is called, *Hold On, Let Go - Facing ALS with Courage and Hope*. And my name is Nadine Sands."

The first time I said it, I started with my name and title. We all practiced reciting our scripts in different ways, and after saying them a few times everyone got better and stronger, but my hard exterior started to crumble. I chose to not participate in the three-minute speech to elaborate on the description of our books at the end of the workshop. I wanted to tell my new friends more, I really did. I'm passionate about our story, about Mike and his incredible attitude and grace in the face of death, but I knew I'd have to tell about his recent passing. Even though I could share that with the people at my table and with a few one on one, I couldn't say it to the whole group—standing at the front with a microphone.

I would have liked to tell the group how my book is based on my ALS With Courage blog and how I felt called to start my blog in order to keep family and friends informed of Mike's brave battle, and how, unexpectedly, it became an excellent outlet for me. I would have said that we clung to faith, hope and love while we let go of everything, and while we let go of everything we gained exceedingly more than we could have imagined. Perhaps I would have told them about a few of my most memorable blog posts (most memorable to me) like, "Mike's Glass is Half Full," "Grasping at Straws," "Hold On and Let Go," and Mike's "Ahoy, Matey." I want them to know that Mike contributed to the blog as well, how he always inspired our readers to keep looking up, and how he made them laugh. I would have explained that while the book is about a courageous guy fighting for his life against a dreadful disease, and the interweaving of joy and grief, it's really mostly about love.

You don't have to go further than the cover to know that my book is a love story. I hope you will judge my book by its cover.

I'm without my Valentine, but not without his lingering love and the incredible, unchangeable, unfathomable love of God. And His mercy carries me.

Facing ALS with courage and hope

hold on, let go

Nadine Sands
with Michael Sands

Bulletproof - Mar 10, 2015

Last week was tough. I was really sad, and I was sick, and then all of a sudden I became anxious, worried and afraid. I was sad for obvious reasons but putting together a blog post of all our accounts of Mike's last days took the sadness to a whole new level. I was sick with the flu, not terribly sick (I still taught my fitness classes) but just sick enough that a few tears from being sad made my head pound and my nose run. I worked hard to keep the tears at bay, but teetered on the edge most of the time.

On Wednesday right after I put an order in for my books, anxiety, worry and fear came. These three weren't subtle and they weren't kind or gentle; they came like bullets or darts or something. I thought, *Sure enough, here I am, the most vulnerable I've ever been, and the devil starts firing. That's just like him.*

Every step of the way I have consulted with God and committed my book to Him. Before and after I decided to write it, before and after I signed with my publisher, before and after the introduction, before and after every paragraph, every chapter, before and after editing, proofreading, typesetting ... every single step, every single word—I consulted with God and committed it to Him. And then when I ordered my books for my upcoming book signing and other events, I froze.

I was gripped with fear wondering what I had done. I was afraid I made a huge mistake. I had thoughts like, *You're not a writer. What do I know and who cares anyway?* My trust in God waned as the negative voices swept in. I hate when that happens! When I shared my feelings with Elanna, she said she knew something was wrong.

With tears in my eyes, I stated, "I'm not an author."

She said, "Yes, you are."

I responded, "I can't do this."

She said, "Yes, you can." Her smile and reassuring words brought me down from the ledge and her prayers washed over me.

In the thick of it I kept telling myself, *This is where Mike would say: "Don't worry, it's going to be okay."* I imagined him putting his hands on my shoulders, pulling me closer—wrapping his strong arms around me and telling me everything was going to be okay. That's how he did it, and even when he became paralyzed his re-assuring look and warm smile held me tight, and everything was always all right.

I now realize the fear wasn't just about my book; it was about my life. Moving forward without Mike is just so heartbreaking; it's disappointing and sometimes scary. He always helped me, he always encouraged me, he prayed for me and reminded me not to worry.

The conversation I had with Elanna really helped, but I still felt a little overwhelmed. That's when I heard God speak. I was pretty sure He said, "Come with Me." So I put my Bible in a backpack and drove to the dike. I didn't go to the dike down the road where we usually go because it's always so busy, especially on such a beautiful day. I went north toward Golden Eagle golf course, which is not much further but felt far away from my worry and fear. I drove to the very end of Ladner Road, turned around at the golf course–a hidden gem off the beaten track, and headed back. Nathan told me about the golf course where a short hike into the woods on the first of a series of mountains leads to a beautiful lake—Goose Lake.

Anyway, I stopped at a dike I'd never been to, not far from there. I walked west on the overgrown path, the Thompson Mountains on my near right and farmland vast on my left. In the very far distance on the other side of that land, I could see a wall of trees that separated the busy world from this wide open, quiet and peaceful refuge I was now in. The wall of trees was kind of hazy from the glow of the sun. I felt far from everyone and really close to God. I just walked and talked with Him. There were a few benches along the way, and I thought I should stop to read my Bible and pray. I felt God say it was okay because His Word was hidden in my heart. And then I was encouraged as the Word in my heart spoke to me:

"We walk by faith, not by sight." (from Corinthians 5:7) "With God all things are possible." (Matthew 19:26) "If He is for us, who can be against us?" (Romans 8:31) "He is able to do immeasurably more than all we ask or imagine." (Ephesians 3:20) "He will surround you with favour as with a shield." (Psalm 5:12) "He goes with you; He will never leave you nor forsake you." (Deuteronomy 31:8) "He knows when you sit down and when you rise up." (Psalm 139:2) "Even the hairs of your head are numbered." (Matthew 10:30) "He hasn't given you a spirit of fear, but of power, love and a sound mind." (2 Timothy 1:7) "I will strengthen you and help you and hold you up with my righteous right hand." (Isaiah 41:10) . . . and on it went.

I eventually sat down with the mountains to my back and my face to the sun. "Be still and know that I am God," (Psalm 46:10) was the next verse to come, so that's what I did. It's the last verse I read when I sat with our old dog, Isla, shortly before she took her last breath. I thought of Mike and how his death reminded me of hers; so peaceful.

Heading back, I felt refreshed, like my thirst had been quenched and my fear had disappeared. Realistically, when all those boxes of my books show up on the doorstep, a little fear might reappear, but it's okay. There are going to be battles but God is with me and He's got me covered. From head to toe, He's got me covered and right where He wants me. And with Mike's positive influence, the prayers of family and friends, God's Word hidden in my heart, His shield around me, and His endless mercy, there's really no need to worry—I am bulletproof!

No Doubt - Mar 21, 2015

Yesterday when I read my daily devotional book *My Utmost For His Highest*, I was encouraged and challenged like most days. The author, Oswald Chambers, says, "A life of faith is not a life of one glorious mountaintop experience after another, like soaring on eagle's wings, but is a life of day-in and day-out consistency, a life of walking without fainting (see Isaiah 40:3)... It is a faith that has been tried and proved and has withstood the test."

Scottish-born Chambers, who, in my head I just call Oswald or OC, has been encouraging me and challenging me through his daily reader for almost two decades. Even though he is long gone from this world, his wisdom and insight live on. The internet was where I learned some of the following information about him. He was only forty-three years old when he died in 1917 from complications after having his appendix removed. Oswald, an artist, minister, teacher, evangelist and chaplain to soldiers in the war, died just before his first book went to print. His wife Gertrude, who Oswald called Biddy, short for the "Beloved Disciple," dedicated the rest of her life to transcribing books from the notes she had taken from Oswald's lectures and sermons. Overall, she published thirty books with her husband's name on each one. *My Utmost for His Highest* is his best seller and a constant source of inspiration in my life.

I have quoted Oswald a lot in my three and a half years of blogging. In the editing phase of *Hold On, Let Go* I had an assignment to obtain permission from certain publishers of certain authors I quoted—Oswald Chambers' publisher was at the top of the list. I was back and forth with a gentleman by the name of Mr. Rock from Discovery House Publishers, who handled such requests. By the end of our interactions, I was very honoured to be granted the permission to use Mr. Chambers' quotes and I considered the very kind and encouraging Mr. Rock a new friend.

Anyway, back to yesterday's reading. Oswald went on to say this about faith: "Living a life of faith means never knowing where you are being led. But it does mean loving and knowing the One who is leading. It is literally a life of faith, not of understanding and reason—a life of knowing Him who calls us to go. Faith is rooted in the knowledge of a Person, and one of the biggest traps we fall into is the belief that if we have faith, God will surely lead us to success in the world."

It would be easy to have faith if having faith guaranteed success, if it meant never facing adversity, if it meant getting what you wanted, but of course that's not how it is.

When Mike was first diagnosed with ALS, a couple of people told me that it couldn't be God's will for Mike to have this terrible illness and that we just needed to keep praying for God's will and Mike would surely be healed. Well, I did pray every day that God would heal Mike, but I also had faith to believe that whether Mike was healed or not we were in God's will, and this is what His will looked like for us right then—whether we liked it or not.

This is faith: believing that there is absolutely nothing God cannot do even when He doesn't save you from ALS (or in Oswald Chambers' case, appendicitis). Walking with Him even when your legs are rendered useless. Trusting Him to make every decision in your life whether you like it or not. Knowing that for those who love Him, all things work together for good (Romans 8:28) and He has your best interest at heart.

This also is faith. Without a shadow of a doubt, He will see you through whatever He leads you to.

God is so much more interested in our souls than our cells. Our physical bodies just house us. Of course, He cares about every aspect of our lives, but He loves who we are inside. Redeeming our souls is His goal. He sent His Son to save the part of us that doesn't perish. The body, along with the ALS or MS or cancer or whatever, just turns back to dust.

"There will come one day a personal and direct touch from God when every tear and perplexity, every oppression and distress, every suffering and pain, and wrong and injustice will have a complete and ample and overwhelming explanation."
Oswald Chambers

"The suffering won't last forever. It won't be long before this generous God who has great plans for us in Christ—eternal and glorious plans they are!—will have you put together and on your feet for good."
1 Peter 5:10 (Message)

CHAPTER 4
Ahoy, Matey—So Long, My Friend

"When your boat is in trouble, you have to keep your eyes on the Lighthouse. The Lighthouse will lead you to a safe landing."
Michael Sands

Journal entry from April 5, 2011

Mike and I had a beautiful prayer time this morning. Part of our reading from Oswald Chambers says, "His agony was the basis for the simplicity of our salvation. The cross of Christ was a triumph for the Son of Man. It was not only a sign that our Lord had triumphed, but that He had triumphed to save the human race. Because of what the Son of Man went through, every human being has been provided with a way of access into the very presence of God." Matthew 26:39 —"Going a little further, He fell with His face to the ground and prayed, My Father, if it is possible, may this cup be taken from me. Yet not as I will, but as You will."

~

This chapter contains one blog post. I originally placed it at the end of Chapter Three, but not only did it make that chapter really long, I think it's just best on its own. Warning: it's heavy. Like the last chapter though, it's about God's mercy and grace and, of course, His impeccable love. But aren't they all? Aren't all the chapters of our lives about those things? For those of us who call God our Father, our Redeemer, our Lighthouse, wouldn't you agree that the chapters of our lives are steeped in God's mercy, grace and love? It's usually when we look back that we notice the most.

Journal entry from Jan 5, 2015 (the day Mike passed away)

I knew Mike was going to die, but I honestly didn't believe it. His passing was peaceful and calm—no gasping for air, no gagging. I think maybe he was gone before he stopped breathing. He stared past me and I wondered if he could see angels, or maybe Jesus. I wondered if he was on his way, but even still I expected him to improve. Our three o'clock in the morning prayer time was beautiful. Our last prayer time together—a gift from God! I prayed with words I didn't choose; words that flowed, like a poem.

Just yesterday, when Mike felt better, he said he wanted to go home. We were getting things ready—oxygen, a nurse, etc., so we could leave. Shortly before that, after settling into his new room on 3 North, he spelled, "It reminds me of Elaine." I listed off all the Seinfeld episodes I could think of with hospital scenes, but I didn't get it. Later, when I told Mike's sister Pat what Mike said about his very small hospital room, she knew exactly. She told me he was referring to the episode where the Chinese food restaurant Elaine really likes won't deliver to her side of the street, so she takes over a janitor's closet in a building across from hers where the restaurant will deliver. When I told Mike that Pat figured it out, he was so happy. We all had a good laugh.

~

If you aren't a Seinfeld fan, that will probably mean nothing to you, but it meant a lot to us. If you know the scene, just imagine a couple of nurses, a doctor, a respirologist and me in a tiny hospital room trying to bring Mike in on his bed and realizing we have to turn the bed around. I looked at him and grinned; we both found it comical. He couldn't wait for the room to clear so he could tell me how he thought of Elaine and her broom closet. It still strikes me funny to this day—Jerry, George and Kramer going over to see her and all squeezing into this little closet with brooms and other equipment while she's waiting for her Chinese food delivery.

Mike was at peace and we were still laughing even down to the final hours before his passing.

Greener on the Other Side - Mar 31, 2015

Here is the account of Mike's final day from the viewpoints of Elanna, Erin, Madison, Nathan and me.

According to Elanna:

I have been holding onto the details of the day as though somehow I could hold onto Mike. I arrived at the hospital on Monday, January 5th, around 9:00 or 9:30 a.m., expecting to help Mike and Nadine get ready to come home. It was clear, however, that Mike wasn't doing as well as the day before. He sort of had a vacant look in his eyes. Just the day before, Mike was saying he was coming home, and we all believed he was. Indeed, he was going home—just not to his earthly home.

According to Erin:

I will never forget the last moments I shared with my dad the day before he died. My mom texted me that morning and said that Dad had gone to the hospital the night before. I remembered when I was at their place that afternoon, he struggled with his breathing and some choking, but this was not out of the ordinary. It was just the two of us alone in his hospital room. I sat and rubbed his warm and soft feet. He had such a glow to his face, despite the fact I knew he had been struggling so hard to breathe. The nurse kept telling him he should take the medication prescribed to help him relax, but he refused. He just kept smiling at me despite his struggle for air.

I told him stories of all the menial things going on in my life. The lady on my strata trying to get me fined for my "tacky decorations" and my latest encounter with the grumpy checkout lady at the grocery store. He didn't once take his eyes off of me and just smiled. He always made me feel like everything I said was important; meanwhile, he was fighting for his life.

We sat together and I just held his fragile body in my arms. Although this certainly wasn't the first time he had been sick and he had gone to the hospital once before, something in my heart knew that his time on earth was coming to an end. Before I left, I kissed his forehead and said, "Thank you." I thanked him for always making me eat my fruit and veggies as a child (and boy did I put up a fight). I thanked him for our walks along Mill Lake, as we secretly threw bread to the geese and watched them battle it out (even though this was strictly prohibited). I thanked him for helping me become a teacher and for always being proud of me. He looked at me and just smiled while we both held back the tears.

According to Me (Nadine):

It was a really nice prayer time together at three o'clock the morning of the day Mike passed away. Among many things, I prayed that the Lord would surround us with angels, and I thanked Him that wherever we were was exactly where we were meant to be. I played one of our playlists from my phone and sang along with the comforting songs, including, "Lord, I need Thee." Mike always wanted me to sing to him, but I don't have a good voice, so I rarely sang. That morning I sang and angels came and we knew peace more than ever before.

At about 5:30 a.m., I told Mike that we should try to get a little more sleep. He agreed, so I laid back down beside him. When I woke up about an hour later, something had changed. He was staring straight ahead. I was unable to read his eyebrows and his blink, so I asked him to look toward the window in response to my questions. Ever so slowly, he moved his eyes toward the window to a series of questions including, "Are you comfortable?" He was. The doctor came and said Mike's potassium levels were low and he needed some saline. I put some through his tube along with some food. I told him he needed to keep his strength up if he wanted to go home later. I knew in my heart that he probably wouldn't be going back to our home that day, but had no idea he'd be going home to heaven.

According to Madison:

I was away playing hockey that weekend and hadn't

had much communication with my mom. I had a feeling deep down something was wrong but tried not to think about it. I got home around seven o'clock Sunday night. Instinctively, the first thing I do every day when I get home is look straight in my dad's direction and greet him. His welcoming smile was my favourite thing. That night when I looked in the direction of his chair and saw it was empty, I knew... I called my mom. She reassured me everything was okay. "Dad is doing better and we hope to come home in the next couple of days. He is sleeping so you can come visit him tomorrow."

That next morning when I got up, the first thing on my mind was Dad. I got dressed, went to the store to find the softest stuffy I could (my dad loved soft touch) and went straight to the hospital. At that moment, I never knew that that stuffed zebra would become the most cherished thing I have.

When I first saw my dad, it was a bit scary. He had an oxygen mask on and he was looking straight ahead. He was unable to make eye contact with me and the tendons in his neck tensed every time he took a breath. Every ounce of his strength I could see was used to breathe. People would have called me crazy, but I still thought he was coming home. I sat down and placed the stuffed zebra on his naked chest so he could feel the soft fur against him and proceeded to tell him, my mom and aunt about my weekend.

According to Elanna:

Around 11:30 a.m. or noon, I told Nadine to run

home for a few minutes to get what she needed and email her publisher with her final book edits. She was reluctant to go, and I kept saying, "Just go, we'll be fine, I'm here and I'll look after him." She finally agreed. Madison went with her. While they were gone, I brushed Mike's hair, got cold cloths for his forehead and sang him some songs. Mike loved all the old hymns, and the one that I kept repeating for this very moment was written by Annie S. Hawks titled "I Need Thee Every Hour."

"I need thee, Oh I need Thee, Every hour I need Thee, O bless me now my Saviour, I come to Thee..."

It was only about half an hour after Nadine left that the nurse came in and checked Mike's vitals. His blood pressure was dropping, and the nurse was giving me "the look." He said to call Nadine to come back right away, as it wouldn't be long. I remember thinking to myself, *This guy doesn't know Mike! Does he even have his nursing certification? He obviously doesn't know what he's talking about.* For four years, we knew this day was coming, but when it presented itself I was strangely shocked.

Nadine was on her way back when I called. A few minutes later she came rushing into the room and Madison soon followed. I called the whole family, and one by one they filtered in—Peter, Erin, Nathan, our parents...

According to Madison:

I went home and packed some things so I could go back to the hospital until I had to go to work. Soon after I left, I got a call. "Madison, you should come to the hospital now." I could tell by the tone in my aunt's voice, it wasn't good. Within minutes I was back at the hospital, and when I ran into the room I could tell there was a drastic decline. I looked straight at my mom and the look on her face was enough to know that this was it. I couldn't tell you what I was feeling; I just instantly lost all strength and dropped to the floor. I began to scream. Feeling nauseous, I started gagging.

Thankfully, my mom was able to get me into the bathroom and calm me down. Head in the toilet, we prayed together that I would gain the strength to be strong for my dad in his last moments. I knew he wouldn't want to hear or see me that way—I quickly calmed down and went back into the room.

According to Me:

Elanna told me what the nurse said. I told Elanna that the nurse didn't know Mike. "Mike's a fighter. He can recover." She replied, "I know." I called Mike's sister, Aileen, to tell her what the nurse said. I put the phone up to Mike's ear so she could say something to him. She told him to hang on and that they would be there the next day. It was only the day before, while on the phone with Aileen and Pat, I asked Mike if his sisters needed to come that night because they couldn't get a flight until two days later. He assured us he was okay, no need to rush … he said it wasn't an emergency.

According to Madison:

I laid down beside my dad on his bed, my head on his chest, holding on tight to the soft, stuffed zebra. I wasn't sure how long it would be, but I knew he was on his way. I found myself gazing at my dad's breathing, listening to my mom singing and talking to him. His breathing was slowly decreasing, becoming less frequent. Soon he became totally still, and his breathing became non-existent. I looked at my mom; both of us knew he was gone. Heaven's gates opened before him.

According to Elanna:

The nurse was right after all; it was Mike's time to go. He didn't struggle, there was no gasping, there was no pain. Mike simply transitioned from this life to the next. It really was a perfect ending and a perfect beginning.

According to Me:

Saying goodbye was surreal. I remember thinking he was on his way, but he could still come back. I remember thinking how surprisingly strong I felt. I remember thinking how good he smelled. There was still a hint of peppermint body wash from the shower Jackie (one of his caregivers) gave him on Saturday. She would have also used the peppermint balm she always rubbed, with so much love, on his neck, shoulders and upper back.

According to Erin:

At the end of our visit on Sunday, I told my dad I would see him tomorrow. Sadly, I only saw his lifeless body—he passed just before I got there. The next time I see him will be in heaven and I can't wait to run around the lake with him and rile up the geese. I love him and miss him more than I could ever express in words.

According to Nathan:

I was at work. I took a quick break to check my phone and I had a message from my aunt. She asked me to call her as soon as possible, but when I did it was too late. She told me my dad had passed away. When I got to the hospital, everyone was gathered around his bed. Less than twenty-four hours earlier, we gathered around his bed, visiting, laughing, talking about him going home. My daughter, Leah, rubbed lotion on his feet.

I held my mom tight. She cried … we all cried, of course, but we laughed a little too. We talked about how my dad, just the day before, made reference to a Seinfeld episode regarding his small hospital room. It took us all a long time to say goodbye. Eventually, we had to leave. We had to walk away and it was the hardest thing we ever did.

Later, at home, I mentioned how impactful it was to see what was left behind—the shell of a man. A shell that housed an unbelievably strong, unbreakable spirit, now free … the difference between the two was so profound.

According to Me:

It rained throughout the night before. It actually poured—it woke us up from our sleep. I unlocked the wheels of Mike's bed and turned it as much as I could toward the window. "Look, Mike, it's pouring rain. Isn't that great?" Mike just loved the sound of the rain and it wasn't until the next day after he had passed away that I thought of something he had mentioned a few times over the years. He told me that W.C. Fields' wife turned the sprinkler on the roof the night Fields lay in bed dying so he could hear for one last time his favourite sound—the sound of the falling rain.

According to Elanna:

I don't think things will ever be the same again. I don't think I will ever fully recover. It seems melodramatic, but Mike was like my own flesh-and-blood brother. We had a secret world of non-verbal communication, suctioning, feeding tubes (and a host of other stuff that comes along with ALS). We knew each other's secrets and had a bond that went beyond the "brother/sister-in-law" norm. I would have done anything for him, and he would have done anything for me.

I am happy for him, as I picture him joyfully moving freely, unencumbered by this earthly shell. At the same time, I am empty, missing my lifetime friend and brother.

Mike made life interesting and fun. He was one of the smartest people I have known. He was funny and he made me laugh and I made him laugh.

According to Me:

We are doing okay most of the time, but the sadness grows thicker, kind of like mud. Sometimes I feel like I'm mucking around, waist deep in it. I know we'll be okay, but we'll never be the same again.

In the afternoon of the day Mike passed away, while we were all sitting together at home, I sat in Mike's chair. All of a sudden I was moving into a reclined position—my granddaughter Leah had the controls. She laid me back, covered me with a blanket, rolled up my pant legs, took off my socks and rubbed lotion on my feet. No words were said. Wow is all I can say now. I'm so choked up thinking about it. It was so precious, and it ministered to me in an extraordinary way.

Leah was five at the time. And when I close my eyes, I see the hands of Jesus on the little hands of Leah directing the flow of hers and His gentle touch of mercy and love on Mike's and then my feet.

I'll finish with a few last words from Mike's post "Ahoy Matey" from July 2013. It's a piece he wrote on return from our trip to the province of Newfoundland and Labrador where we were to watch Madison play in the World Ball Hockey tournament:

"I was diagnosed with ALS in 2011. When someone tells you, you've got two to five years to live, one's fear instinct kicks in. Anyone who says they're not afraid when first diagnosed is just fooling themselves. Even General George S. Patton, who had ice in his veins when staring down his enemies, stated, "If we take the generally accepted definition of bravery as a quality which knows no fear, I have never seen a brave man. All men are frightened. The more intelligent they are, the more they are frightened." But you can't stay in fear mode forever; you have to go on living. Like the captain of the HMS Newfoundlander and so many of the seamen who stared death in the face while on the high seas, they had to carry on.

"The secret to getting yourself through trying times is to get yourself in the right frame of mind. In The Wizard of Oz, the cowardly lion needed the Wizard to give him a medal in order to put him in the proper mindset to face his fears. I look to God to get me in the right frame of mind to face this dire diagnosis. In nautical terms, God is THE Lighthouse. When your boat is in trouble, you have to keep your eyes on the Lighthouse. THE Lighthouse will lead you to a safe landing.

"Eventually, all bad things must come to an end. There is a rainbow at the end of the storm. The rainbow may not be a cure for ALS, or a sudden reversal of symptoms. But if you have the belief, like I have the belief, that something grand awaits us after this life, then there is nothing to fear. So, I wait, knowing that my faith is being sure of what I hope for (taken from a plaque in my bedroom).

"P.S. One last Newfie joke that I remember from when I was a kid: Did you hear about the Newfie who was killed while ice fishing? Yeah, he was run over by a Zamboni at centre ice of Maple Leaf Gardens. Corny, yes, but it brings a nostalgic smile to my face every time."

Mike having fun shopping while in Newfoundland and Labrador.
There was rarely a dull moment.

The Lord held us up. Thanks to Elanna for capturing this moment in
Newfoundland and Labrador.

CHAPTER 5
Spaghetti and Words That Make You Squirm

*"He escorts me to the banquet hall; it's obvious how much
He loves me..."*

Song of Songs 2:4 (NLT)

Say Cheese - April 10, 2015

Girl/boy communication was so simple in grade four, don't you think? A young girl had a crush on a classmate, so she wrote her feelings on a piece of paper torn from one of her notebooks. She folded it up into a little square and gave it to a trusted friend to deliver to the lucky young lad at recess or lunch.

It's like my heart is full of blank pages these days, like a notebook. I pour my deepest feelings on those pages and then tear them out. I fold them into little squares and give them to God, my trusted Friend, and ask Him to deliver them to Mike up there in heaven.

On Friday night, the night before my book signing, I went to bed with a bit of a knot in my stomach and an ache in my head. I'm not fond of going to bed without Mike as it is, like I've shared before, but this night I missed him more than ever. Instead of climbing right in under my cozy covers, I got down on the floor.

Amongst all the boxes of books, on my knees, I prayed over them. I prayed over all my books like I had done every day since receiving them, and I prayed about the book signing and I prayed about many things. Eventually, my face was on the floor and I just agonized that I had to move forward without Mike ... that he's not here with me anymore.

It's popular to believe that our loved ones are looking down on us from heaven, but I'm not convinced of it. The Bible says that there are no tears in heaven; there is no sadness, sorrow or pain. That's one reason I don't think he can see me. I think he's enamoured with Jesus and enjoying many great things.

So, I came up with the idea that because I talk to God, and because Mike is in His presence, Mike and I can communicate through Him. I understand if you are tempted to roll your eyes right about now, but I researched it and found I'm not the only one who thinks this way. There are a number of ideas. This one is mine and I'm sticking with it.

The first note Mike wrote me almost twenty-eight years ago was kind of magical. When I close my eyes, I can see myself standing in his crowded kitchen at "the Shack" where he lived with a bunch of guys. I had little black ears on the top of my head, whiskers drawn on my face and a tail attached to my backside. I can't remember any other Halloween costumes that night except for mine—my simple and cute mouse costume. One of Mike's friends handed me a note explaining why he wasn't there. He had to work. It was folded a bunch of times into a little square and it accompanied a piece of cheese. The cheese was wrapped and tied with a bit of string.

Mike captured my heart that night with a little piece of cheese, a note and some string. He pursued me and it didn't take long before I was his. He continued to woo me throughout our marriage with his simple and sometimes silly messages of love.

Shortly after Mike passed away, my friend Carolyn from school came up to me one night before class began. I could see she had something for me and struggled a little to explain. She said she had something she wanted to give me from her baby daughter's things. Her daughter passed away a number of years ago when she was just a few months old. Carolyn said she really felt like she was supposed to give this special something to me, and then when she read my blog about the rocks she knew for sure. She handed me the gift and told me it was a message from Mike. With tears welling up in my eyes, I slowly removed the tissue paper it was wrapped in and revealed a rock. Engraved in the rock are the words "You are loved."

I'm so glad Mike is free, but the selfish me wants him back. I'd take just a day—there are things I want to say. So, I write them down on those pages in my heart. I tear them out and fold them into little squares and get my trusted Friend to pass them on to him.

P. S. The night after I received the note and gift-wrapped cheese, Mike and I sat beside each other on his couch and watched a movie. There was a bunch of us crammed on the couch and we all shared a big blanket. Mike's and my hidden hands were inches away from each other, and by the end of the movie our fingers were interlocked. When we used to tell the story, Mike would say, "She took my hand." And I would say, "He took mine." So, my dear Michael, let's agree, we took each other's hand. And the rest is history.

From my journal (all from 2011)

June 27: When I woke up, Mike asked if he could hold my hand. He took one of my hands in both of his and told me that he loved me so much. What a wonderful way to start the day!

March 10: I didn't sleep well. At 3:00 a.m. I was fully awake, reeling about some mistakes I've made like quitting a good job and other things. Mike encouraged me and told me it's a test of my faith. He prayed for me.

March 14: I spent most of the day in bed with the flu. Mike read to me from the Bible, sitting in a chair in the hall (he said he didn't want to catch what I have). He read random verses to me … beautiful verses including Philippians 4:4-7: "Rejoice in the Lord always. I will say it again: Rejoice! Let your gentleness be evident to all. The Lord is near. Do not be anxious about anything, but in every situation, by prayer and petition, with thanksgiving, present your requests to God. And the peace of God which transcends all understanding will guard your hearts and your minds in Christ Jesus." (NIV)

March 18: It's almost like his first thought of the day is, How can I make her smile?

March 31: Mike wanted to start the prayers tonight. He said he wanted to pray for me because I never pray for myself.

April 8: As I lay in bed this morning and prayed in my head, Mike, still sleepy, turned over and put his arm around me. I thought, Two peas in a pod. We fit together perfectly!

May 15: Mike prayed for me for peace and all the other words on the rocks in my garden.

July 31: I dreamt that Mike rolled over in bed and told me there was an angel beside me. When I told Mike about the dream, he said I had it wrong and that the angel was beside him. Mike calls me his angel and other lovely things.

~

Those are just a few examples from my journal of the kind of caregiver and encourager Mike was. Even after his diagnosis and right up until the end, he never said "Woe is me." He cared about my well-being and the well-being of others to the best of his ability … at every stage of his illness … at every stage of our lives together.

There are many accounts in that journal of me and Mike spending time in bed together—reading, praying, talking, being intimate. Although the circumstances were so sad and so difficult, the unexpected, unhurried time we had together was an absolute gift!

Journal entry from March 20, 2011

Oswald Chambers says, "The reason for asking is so you may get to know God better. For your Father knows the things you have need of before you ask Him (Matthew 6:8). We should keep praying to get a perfect understanding of God Himself." Mike and I had a beautiful start to the day—praying, reading, making love—as the sun shone through the window. Mike told me I was beautiful. I simply said, "Thank you." I usually find it hard to accept Mike's compliments (or any compliments for that matter).

To accept and reply "Thank you" will now be my new response. And I will cherish all the lovely, kind words from day one.

~

I'm just going to pause right here to make sure we are on the same page. Since I started writing about us, I've stopped mid-story along the way a few times to remind my readers that although I mostly write about the love and keep it positive, things weren't always great. It wasn't all sunshine and roses. Most married people will know this. It was a good marriage, but like all couples we experienced highs and lows. Our past has some ugly stuff like everyone else's does. There were a few times in our marriage where I wondered who was packing their bags because one of us had to leave. You get to your wit's end and then you get on your knees. Thankfully, God always responded so graciously.

I haven't written much about our trials pre-ALS because I only started writing about us post-diagnosis. During this time, our love for each other and our love for the Lord rose to new heights and broke record depths, and that's what I focus on most.

Here's the thing. There's this mundane side of marriage that we all need to embrace. If it were always romantic, there would be no such thing. Instead, it's a plugging along, hitting the snooze button, getting the laundry done, rushing to work, driving the kids around kind of thing; the list goes on. In the busiest times of life, you might feel like two ships passing in the night. But every once in a while, you stop for a minute and realize the rouse of butterflies, tingling in your thighs, a twinkle in your beloved's eye; you do have a love life!

Spaghetti and Quickies - April 18, 2015

I love love. Happy couples make me smile. My favourite movies are the ones where the boy gets the girl and they live happily ever after. In real life, we know that "happily ever after" doesn't exist. Good relationships take a lot of work and sometimes those couples are happy, sometimes sad, sometimes mad and sometimes simply perfect.

A few years into our marriage, I thought I had it all figured out. I quickly caught on to the secret of a happy relationship. I realized that if I put my husband before myself and committed my life to making him happy, he would be happy. And if he was happy and had all his needs met, he'd reciprocate. Simple, right? In theory it's simple; in reality, not so much. It's a little more complicated than that, especially when you're kind of selfish like me.

Mike was easy to please; a plate of spaghetti and a "quickie" and he was more than happy. I wasn't that easy. I'm not talking about spaghetti and quickies, not at all because: A) I'm gluten-free so I don't eat spaghetti, and B) quickies are for men. I think most of the time, women enjoy going slow when it comes to sex. What I mean is, I was more difficult to please. Maybe I was more selfish than he was. And even though in my heart I believed my "put him first" plan was the best way to a successful marriage, I often veered from "the plan" with the attitude, *What about me?*

Throughout my marriage when I struggled with "the plan," I prayed that the Lord would help me. But serving others and denying yourself doesn't always come easy. So, I continued to pray and, well, you know what they say—be careful what you wish for. In March of 2011, God whispered, "Here's your opportunity."

With God's help and the help of family and home care support, I joyfully served my husband unselfishly for almost four years while his health declined from the effects of ALS. I didn't really have a choice in taking care of him, but I had a choice in the "joyfully" part, although Mike made it pretty easy and I definitely clung to the Lord. It was a challenge every single day and sometimes I thought I might break. It's bizarre how only three and a half months have gone by since Mike passed away and I've already forgotten how taxing caring for a man with ALS can be.

I guess I could say my plan worked. I put Mike first and met all of his needs to the best of my ability. He was happy and his happiness made me happy. Mike had an awesome attitude regardless, which was helpful, and I gave thanks for that every day. I was in awe and I was so humbled.

He was so thankful. I remember telling him not to waste his precious breath and energy thanking me so much. Thinking about his look of gratitude melts my heart. He was so grateful and so patient with me.

I say, "Thank you for making my job as easy as possible, Michael Sands. Thank you for making me laugh in the grief and for smiling at me when I was at my wit's end." And he would probably say, "Thanks for all the spaghetti and quickies. And thanks for denying yourself and serving me … you did a good job!"

I've stated a few times how happy I am Mike's free. He probably thinks the same thing about me. I can barely type this statement without losing it because I would have taken care of him for fifty more years. Oh, my goodness, I miss him so much!

Sex, Hugs, Rock & Soul - April 30, 2015
The inspiration for my last blog post came from an invitation I received from Wendy Toyer, Executive Director of the ALS Society of B.C. She asked me if I would speak at the dinner of an upcoming ALS golf tournament fundraiser. A portion of the proceeds raised go to caregiver programs, so every year they ask a caregiver to share.

I've had "caregiver" on my mind since then and what it meant to me to be Mike's caregiver. I really poured out my heart in that last post and struck a chord with many, and perhaps a nerve or two with a few.

My friend Pauline said, "This was lovely, Nadine—poignant and just a little risqué, too. Well done! Your writing just gets better and better with each post. You are a gifted artist. Must be all the love spilling over into brilliance. Thank you for sharing your journey and for keeping Mike's memory alive for those who he meant so much to."

I appreciate all the comments I get regarding my blog posts. They help me connect with my readers and they help me grow as a writer and as a person. When I read Pauline's comment, I thought, *Yes, it's risqué!* But I wasn't necessarily going for that when I wrote it. I could have just as easily called it "Hot Dogs and Head Rubs." The point that I was making was that Mike was easy to please throughout our marriage pre-ALS, and his easy and upbeat attitude helped make it a joy to take care of him post-diagnosis.

Anyway, my "risqué" blog post got more hits in a twenty-four-hour period than any other post, with the exception of the posts Mike and I each wrote during the ALS Ice Bucket Challenge last August. So, I guess a risqué title draws people in. I'll have to keep that in mind for next time. Seriously though, here is what's important; we made a deeper connection, you and me, not because of the risqué title but because of the raw content. Being somewhat transparent seems to be appreciated. Here I am, more window, less wall.

Some friends have asked me how it feels to open the curtains so people can see right in. My response has been something like this: When you feel called to share your story, you have to surrender it. Obviously, there are many things I don't share. Even though Mike and I were both really private people, together we agreed at a certain point to surrender our story and not hold back too much, which would hopefully help others—not just those with ALS, but anyone experiencing tough times such as discouragement, disease, depression, impending death and so on.

At some point, you surrender. It's not about you anymore or touchy subjects … it's about others. It's about mothers, daughters, sons, fathers, sisters, and brothers who, too, have had their world cave in for one reason or another. To encourage just one, or to inspire a couple to keep going and not give up! To have faith, to be hopeful, to trust God, to rise above when you feel like digging a hole and jumping in, to give thanks in every ugly circumstance and to keep going.

"He lifted me out of the slimy pit, out of the mud and mire; He set my feet on a rock and gave me a firm place to stand."

Psalm 40:2 (NIV)

Here's a comment I received after my last blog post:

"Beautifully written! I am a social worker with ALS patients and sex can be a difficult topic for some to discuss as ALS changes develop. Thanks for addressing this!"

I returned a message to this social worker, telling her that I very briefly touched on the subject in the last chapter of my book, *Hold On, Let Go*. Mike and I thought it was important to share that even in the final stages of ALS, there was still a physical aspect to our relationship. Although I really missed being hugged, kissed and caressed, we never lost intimacy. It drastically changed, of course, but was never lost. Praise God!

A few other comments:

"Very inspiring, Nadine. Following this has given me some peace in a way I didn't anticipate. Even though it has been twelve years since my mother passed from ALS; in a strange way, seeing how others face this horrible disease with such courage lets me know our family and my mom were not alone. She had to have been so scared, yet she never complained or asked why me. Mike was lucky to have you as his caretaker. Incredibly difficult task few can do."

"ALS will bring the most courageous person to their knees because you feel so helpless to do anything for the person you love. God gives you strength you didn't know you had to finish a journey you never wanted to go on. I miss my wife so much it makes my heart ache with each passing day. God bless!"

"Hey, Nadine, I wanted to tell you that I really appreciated reading your book. It hit home with me. I can only imagine how much effort and emotion and sleepless nights it took. You both have inspired me to see what is important in life and to stay strong. Best wishes to you and your family. Thanks, Scott."

Scott, a friend, was diagnosed with "probable" ALS on February 21, 2013. I went to school with him and his brother. They both showed up at my book signing at Save-On-Foods. Scott and his wife Sandra came first. When I said goodbye to the person ahead of them and then looked up and saw Scott standing right in front of me, I was speechless and wondered if I should say something like *You're so brave*. I didn't say it, but that's what I was thinking. When his brother Neil came, not much was said again. We just kind of looked at each other and knew.

Mike and I both agreed, if our story encouraged or inspired someone or helped someone know they weren't alone, it would be well worth sharing.

When I wrote Spaghetti and Quickies, I had no intention of bringing up sex and ALS. I was simply talking about the realities of marriage and the blessings of being Mike's primary caregiver. And just for the record, while quickies are usually a reality of busy, tired married people, Mike and I made lovemaking (not the quickie kind) a priority.

The details of a couple's love life are personal, private, secret, even sacred, understandably. But why do we often squirm when just the word sex is mentioned? Physical intimacy in a healthy relationship is as natural as breathing; it's vital to the life of the marriage union. Unfortunately, this beautiful, amazing, wonderful, uncomfortable-to-discuss gift from God often gets swept under the rug because it simply feels awkward to talk about.

One day during the time Mike was rapidly becoming paralyzed, someone really close to him started asking me certain questions. It took me a couple of minutes to realize what they were getting at.

I asked right out, "Are you wanting to know if he's still getting it?"

"Yes!" was her reply, obviously relieved that I had guessed. I appreciated the curiosity and that she cared so much to broach the uncomfortable subject. She was relieved to hear me respond "Yes!" and explained she was happy to know Mike had something to look forward to when almost everything else was being lost. She knew it would help with his mental health and emotional wellness.

Because it's primarily involuntary muscles that are involved with sexual arousal and because ALS attacks voluntary muscles, many ALS patients are able to have sex. Often times though, other challenges interfere, like medications, depression, respiratory problems, fatigue, muscle tightness or spasms, caregiver exhaustion and grief (primary caregivers are usually the spouse), and the list goes on. Anyone interested can find more on the internet.

Mike was able, willing and interested a lot. I, on the other hand, was usually exhausted, preoccupied with many thoughts, juggling a lot of things, and grieving. Often, I hoped and prayed he wouldn't give me the look. But when he did, I mustered up all I had and relied on God to give me what it took. Of course, he understood when I just couldn't. Mike had to give up most things he enjoyed, but praise the Lord, He still had this, right up until a couple of weeks before he died. And it sure taught me a lot about the deep recesses of intimacy and love.

"As we live in God, our love grows more perfect."
1 John 4:17 (NLT)

CHAPTER 6
Don't Quit and Remember Your Deodorant

"I can do all things through Him who strengthens me."
Philippians 4:13 (ESV)

Words He Lived By - May 20, 2015

Madison and I are almost done our four-week practicum for the SETA program (Special Education Teacher Assistant, also known as Education Assistant or EA) and are both thoroughly enjoying it. We didn't choose what school we would be at, but we are both pleased with where we were placed. You could definitely tell on Friday afternoon which one of us was at a high school and which one was at an elementary school. I wore black capri pants, a white blouse, a jean jacket and a pair of Vans. Madison had stickers on her face and was wearing a neon shirt, rainbow pants and running shoes—it was Fun Day at her school and the theme was rainbows.

During Christmas break when I suggested to Mike that I not return to the SETA program and perhaps finish at a later date, he replied with the words he lived by, "Don't quit!" He spelled it out a few times over the course of a couple of weeks. It's a statement he modeled every day since he was diagnosed with ALS and ever since I met him, actually.

Mike always delighted in the things I did. He always encouraged me and believed in me. There were even a few times I was mad at him for not stopping me from pursuing something that didn't lead to a successful ending. But looking back now, it was all successful to him because even if I failed, I grew. Success to him was becoming the woman I am and the woman I'm yet to be. I guess he thought the accomplishments, the mistakes, and everything in between were all pretty great because it's what's shaped me into me. And he just loved me incredibly.

Anyway, I'm so glad I didn't quit, not for the obvious reason that I am so close to being done but because Mike would be so proud of me. He'd say, "See, I told you, you could do it."

It's kind of weird how life goes on. Every day that comes and goes from when Mike passed away is another day further away from him. I feel like I just let go of him and now all this time and space separates us. He's all orientated in his new place, and life here on Earth moves on. I wish time could stop for a little while to keep the distance from growing. [My friend Karen, as wise as she is, after reading this paragraph expressed, "Funny, I would think you would think with every passing day, you're one day closer to seeing him again." That put a huge smile on my face. That is a beautiful perspective and that's how I think of it now.]

When Mike passed, I got this glimpse of heaven, and for a couple of weeks after, everything here seemed so ridiculous. Everything paled in comparison to that little glimpse of heaven. I remember lying on Mike's reclining chair, listening to the TV and thinking, *Really? This is so dumb!* Everything seemed dumb. When I had fully returned to Earth, all of a sudden my life became smaller and my purpose became larger. It just seems more important than ever to make my life count and to make Mike proud. With almost everything I do, I think, *Would this make Mike happy?*

In one of the first journal entries after Mike's diagnosis, I wrote: *Mike is worried he will leave me broke.* Thankfully, Mike had a good job as a nurse and was provided with disability and healthcare benefits for the remainder of his life. But we weren't prepared insurance-wise for his demise. Plus, we were in a lot of debt at the time. But God moved mountains in our finances. He provided in such unexpected and remarkable ways. Over the course of those three years and ten months, He definitely put Mike's mind at ease by showing him He'd always provide for me and that I was going to be okay financially.

When Mike and I talked about me registering for the Education Assistant program, we both agreed I should seriously consider it. It was a career I had contemplated for years and planned on investigating more when Madison graduated from high school. Mike got sick before Madison graduated, so I didn't really think about it again until Madison came home from university and said she was interested in it. She had changed her mind about the program she was enrolled in at the university she attended in Calgary, Alberta. Plus, it was tough being away from home, knowing her dad wasn't going to be around for long. So she left university and her ice hockey scholarship behind, with the plan to sign up for the EA program being offered at the local community college. Mike and I both felt it was the right time for me to go as well.

We were eligible for a few more hours of home care support and I was able to move the existing hours around a bit to accommodate my course schedule (a few hours, three evenings a week and most Saturdays). By this time, we had established an excellent team of consistent care providers who knew Mike well and were like family. Elanna happily agreed to give Mike his tube feeds and was there most of the time to oversee things. I never would have given it a second thought if Mike didn't have exceptional care and help.

I'm sure Mike felt useful helping me with homework. I practiced presentations with him and he just smiled the whole time. I remember after a presentation on a sensitive topic, we both cried. His pride and participation meant the world to me! I'm sure it brought him a lot of joy having this opportunity to help me and support me when he was always on the receiving end of those things. Not only that; it seemed he felt a greater sense of peace knowing I was going to be an EA—decent pay, excellent holidays and benefits. I had only ever worked as a self-employed fitness instructor during the course of our marriage, which was and still is a great part-time job. But this new career provided stability for years to come.

Someone, a loved one out of the blue two years after Mike

had passed, sent me a message about me going back to school. She suggested it was bad timing and asked if I had any regrets. Considering Mike had already been gone for quite a while and my mom had just passed, I was confused and upset. Her question and concerns were reasonable, I guess, but perhaps not the best timing. I replied, saying I had no regrets. I assured her that if we didn't have the outstanding care we had and my sister right there, I never would have done it.

I'm not exempt from regret; I've got some. Believe me, I still lose sleep sometimes wondering if I did everything I could to accommodate Mike. I've tossed and turned, questioning if I advocated for him to the very best of my ability. Did I listen with the patience of Job? With the patience of Jesus? Listening to someone who can't speak takes a lot of energy; did I always give him my full attention? Did he always feel heard? I'm afraid, probably not. This kind of regret comes with the territory of being a primary caregiver. I try to give it to God, but obviously it's a process.

The day Mike went into hospital, two days before he died, I had been at school. I came home and he was struggling, choking on saliva, which wasn't unusual. I did as much as I could suction-wise and suggested we go to the pros to get the deeper suctioning he needed. After a few hours, Mike agreed. I honestly don't regret being at school that day; Mike had Jackie.

Jackie adored Mike and he adored her. She gave him the longest, hottest showers, as per order. She took it a step further with an amazing head rub, shoulder and neck massage. She massaged his arms and legs after he was dried off and back in his chair. I'd return to the very familiar scent of peppermint rub and Old Spice body wash and ask how the spa was. Mike would always give me the look of "two thumbs up." Even on this last "spa" day with Jackie while I was doing some aggressive suctioning and everything I could to manage the phlegm and his coughing, I paused to ask him how his time with Jackie was. It was two thumbs up, like always.

Others gave him the same above love. His caregivers treated him like a king … and a friend. When I'd return from evening classes, I'd find Mike and Jon watching hockey or basketball or whatever game was on. Shannon sang and Shuna was always laughing; they all laughed a lot. Raman was quiet and lovely. They were all terrific. I know a few of them confided in Mike, sharing problems and difficulties. He was such a good listener and his look of empathy and love was like a little bit of balm on a painful wound. He was a nurse through and through, right to the end.

It took a lot of persistence and it tried my patience to get that kind of care. For a long time, I constantly called the company to explain again and again that a non-verbal paralyzed man needed (and deserved) the best, consistent care possible. And that's what he eventually received; a priceless gift indeed!

Be Bold - June 16, 2015

They say, "Never let them see you sweat," but that's pretty much impossible for me. Not only do I have overactive sweat glands, but it's been really hot lately. So needless to say, I was sweating bullets while delivering my valedictorian speech at our graduation ceremony last week. Even though speaking in public is getting slightly more comfortable, I'm sure there will always be a little fear and some perspiration.

It started with my speech at Librarian's Night at the House of James bookstore in Abbotsford B.C.— that was a good start. It was short and sweet … well, bittersweet, but it led to book sales and a speaking engagement in March for the Apologetics Canada Conference in Abbotsford.

The next one was for the Richmond ALS Golf Tournament dinner for caregivers. I said a little something and read some of Mike's obituary. Then I said a little more and read my recent blog post, "Spaghetti and Quickies." There was some laughter and quite a few tears, and during most of it you could have heard a pin drop. I remember thinking, *Wow, I'm stronger than I thought.* That is, until I finished and everyone stood up and clapped, and my legs almost gave out on me as I made my way back to my seat beside Elanna, who was there to kind of catch me.

The night after that I spoke at the Riverside Church's women's "Be Brave" event. That was a longer speech. I originally told Ingrid, who invited me, that I wouldn't be able to speak for twenty-five or thirty minutes. Turns out I was wrong. I worked on this speech for a long time and when all was said and done, I struggled to keep it in the timeframe. I called it "Worrier to Warrior."

Then came my speech for graduation a week later. When I heard that my classmates nominated me to say something, I was honoured. I really wanted to say no because it seemed like too much. Then I decided to be braver than I thought I could be.

Strength, courage and confidence are the words

Eleanor Roosevelt uses to explain what we gain when we look fear in the face. She says, "We must do that which we think we cannot."

We all experience fear, and sometimes it stops us and sometimes it doesn't. My recent speaking engagements were scary, and even though I've done some speaking in the past at a few events for my mom and dad's society, Project Wellness, as well as some ladies' church things, this was different. This is about me and Mike and our journey, and now my journey without him. I had to expose my soul, and even though I do that sometimes in my blog, there was nowhere to hide. I had to stand up there in front of everyone.

"No power on earth or in hell can conquer the Spirit of God living within the human spirit. It creates an inner invincibility... The moment we recognize our complete weakness and our dependence upon Him will be the very moment that the Spirit of God will exhibit His power."
Oswald Chambers

Lately I've had to be really brave, but I'm not an expert on bravery—far from it. I've actually failed at being brave a lot. Here's a time. I was nineteen. Two months after I had returned home from Bible College, I got pregnant. Instead of telling my parents or my sister or anyone, Mike and I ran off and got married. Mike would have done whatever I wanted. He didn't want to run away; I did. I didn't really look like I was pregnant for months, so I was able to keep it under wraps for a while. But eventually baby Erin was born and, well, the math doesn't lie. I apologized to my family at some point for not being honest, and of course, I was long forgiven. I still feel badly for running off without telling them.

On June 24th, it will be twenty-seven years since we made that bold decision. It wasn't the greatest start, but it's not really how you start that matters as much as how you finish (just like in life). I think we finished really well. I don't think it could have been a stronger finish. And, of course, there were many, many amazing moments, days and years in between!

P.S. I'd like to say a huge thank you to our local Member of Parliament, Randy Kamp, for delivering my book to Prime Minister Stephen Harper. The Prime Minister sent me a beautiful thank you letter in which he wrote, "By sharing your family's experience with ALS, and the loss of your husband, Michael, you are raising awareness and understanding of the debilitating effects of the disease. I commend your strength in sharing your personal journey and trust that others will find hope in this volume. Please know that it will have a special place in my personal library to remind me that each day is a gift to be cherished."

From Father's Day to our Anniversary - July 4, 2015

The grief was pretty intense from June 21 to the end of June 24—Father's Day to our anniversary. It started before Father's Day, though. I guess a little preparation was going on inside of me, getting me ready for full-blown ugly crying. It gets harder to be apart from Mike with every day that passes, but of course, that's what missing someone is all about. And all the "firsts" are really tough, too.

I've been working on a poem for Mike about all the "firsts" without him. You know, like the first smell of barbecue. We'd both take a deep breath in through the nose to get the most of that first smell of outdoor grilled steak. We'd look at each other and smile and comment on the fantastic aroma. But this year at the first smell of BBQ, I just sighed.

All the firsts are difficult … the first Valentine's Day without him, our kids' and other family birthdays, Easter, Mother's Day, the first Stanley Cup playoffs, the first Father's Day, our anniversary and so on.

My heart may be broken, but at the same time it's absolutely full. The love of family and friends, the prayers, encouraging messages and even gifts are incredible. But more than that, God's perfect love and strong presence in my life holds me up and the joy of the Lord is my strength.

During my dark days between Father's Day and our anniversary, I talked to Pat on the phone. We were discussing plans for a summer visit (me going there). She had no idea how low I was feeling, and I didn't say. I smiled when I heard her cheerful voice. She told me about all the dimes she had been finding lately and made me laugh out loud regarding the dime she saw under the bench at the bus stop on her way home from work. She had to get down on her knees in her nurse's uniform and reach for it. She said she wondered what the other lady there waiting for the bus was thinking, but she didn't care. She felt the dime was a little gift from her little brother. She also shared that while outside on her driveway, playing with her two-year-old granddaughter, she found a dime. She told her granddaughter it was from Uncle Michael.

Her granddaughter replied, "Thank you, Uncle Michael!"

This is the same sweetie pie who said, when told Uncle Michael passed away, "He all better now."

Journal entry from March 25, 2011

I was getting ready for my fitness class when I went into our room to get dressed and saw Mike sitting on the bed with his arms raised (it's part of his exercises). I made a comment about him praising the Lord. He said that God had healed him … and if He chooses not to heal him physically, that's okay. He declared he was in God's hands and that was the best place to be.

Journal entry from April 10, 2011

Today's devotional reading from the Blackaby's *Experiencing God, Day by Day* says, "No illness can defeat us. No disaster can rob us of eternal life. Death can temporarily remove us from those we love, but it transfers us into the presence of the One who loves us most. God's glory is His presence. Death, our greatest enemy, is nothing more than the vehicle that enables believers to experience God's glory!"

Henry Blackaby and Richard Blackaby

CHAPTER 7
My Other Sheila with the Gift of Gab and a Great Laugh

"But those who hope in the Lord will renew their strength.
They will soar on wings like eagles."
Isaiah 40:31 (NIV)

It intrigues me how an all-loving, all-powerful, completely sovereign God, allows such pain and suffering in this world, and yet cares so deeply for each one of us. I wonder how He can endure such sorrow. How can He, compassionate and loving beyond our understanding, watch the atrocities of this world—the injustices, the violence, disease, poverty, war and more, and not completely fall apart? Of course He's God and He's not going to fall apart. He actually holds everything together, but He created us and loves us with a greater love than we can fathom; talk about a broken heart.

There's a certain broken hearts club that only parents know of; the pain and suffering of a child can be excruciating. Grandparents, aunties and uncles are often a part of this club too. As a mother, I have lost sleep, I've wept, I've worried, I've prayed, I've paced, I've begged when any of my children have experienced pain and/or suffering; and their increasing age doesn't change things.

Our Heavenly Father can relate to our pain. He knows sorrow better than anyone. Most of us have asked Him how He could allow this or that terrible thing to happen. Meanwhile, He watched His Son Jesus die a harrowing death, carrying all the sins of the world on Himself, and nailed to a cross.

He's all-knowing of pain and suffering. It makes total sense that He's called "Refuge" numerous times in the Bible. Here is one example: "God is our refuge and strength, an ever-present help in trouble." Psalm 46:1 (NIV) I love how it's worded in the Message Bible: "God is a safe place to hide, ready to help when we need him."

He is also called "Merciful Father" and "source of all comfort," like in this next verse: "All praise to God, the Father of our Lord Jesus Christ. God is our merciful Father and the source of all comfort. He comforts us in all our troubles so that we can comfort others. When they are troubled, we will be able to give them the same comfort God has given us." 2 Corinthians 1:3-4 (NLT)

Trials and troubles in varying degrees are pretty much a guarantee for every human being. But the Bible is full of adjectives that describe a God with extremely broad shoulders. He's a Father exceedingly compassionate and passionate about the consolation of His children. Abba, Father, Dad—a place to run to; a shelter from the storms of life. He knows your broken heart and every tear you've cried.

The Psalmist David writes, "You keep track of all my sorrows. You have collected all my tears in your bottle. You have recorded each one in your book." Psalm 56:8 (NLT)

I often think of Mike's parents when they received the news that their son, their youngest child of five, had ALS.

What went through their minds? I have no idea. Well, I guess I have an idea—despair, helplessness, perhaps? It's in a parent to make their child better or to somehow alleviate their pain, regardless of the child's age. "Inflict me God, not him."

Spread Your Wings and Fly - Aug 4, 2015

All of a sudden, I realized something was missing in my life; I felt so parched, like I hadn't sipped water in days and at the same time I was ready to burst. I guess you could compare it to feeling like a caged bird. Have you ever felt that way? Like your wings were tied to your side—eager to fly but totally grounded? I haven't written anything for a while now and that's how I have felt—grounded. I have lacked energy and motivation. Not just in my writing—in everything. But today is a new day and here I am typing. Even though I'm only a few sentences in, I feel my wings expanding ... *Is it time to fly?* I ask myself. And right away, I'm struck with doubt. I'm wondering if anyone is even interested anymore; I'm questioning myself, *Has your story fizzled? Have your highs and lows become a bore?* Although I feel like I'm just getting started, perhaps this whole writing thing has run its course. I say to myself, *You're a writer; ignore the doubts and keep going.* And the cage door is opened; and I'm free to start soaring.

Speaking of soaring, I am moving. I am spreading my wings and flying a whole two and a half kilometers away. I definitely have mixed emotions about it but accept that "mixed emotions" are just a regular part of my life. Maybe not so much mixed emotions; rather, a rollercoaster ride of emotions … you know, up, down and all around. As a recent example, last Thursday I removed subjects from my new apartment, a beautiful apartment with a lovely view of the Fraser River in a local neighbourhood I heard calling my name. A few hours later, I got word that my mother-in-law had passed away.

Sheila passed away two weeks before the trip the kids and had booked to Toronto to see her and the rest of the family. The trip has been postponed. I had a little collection of goodies to take her: some of Mike's old essays, stories and cards he had written and some crosswords he had saved for her from years ago. Mike used to always collect the crossword puzzles from the newspaper for his mum. He did the crossword himself every day from his newspaper and had my mom and dad save the crossword from theirs. He put them in a box in the dining room closet and took them to his mum when he went to visit every year. She loved it. She stated that once she got started on her crosswords, she couldn't stop. She said she would take some to bed with her, and before she knew it the sun was up, and she hadn't slept a wink. I also have a Christmas tree ornament I made for her with one of Mike's dimes from his coin collection. I have an "I Like Mike" t-shirt from this year's ALS walk and a few other special things I know she would have loved.

Things, of course, mean nothing to her now. She's in the presence of the Lord and reunited with her beloved Michael. When I heard of her passing, I said to my girls who were with me at the time, "I bet your dad saw his mum and asked her what she was doing there so fast. He would have just blinked." I'm sure it was an extremely joyful reunion. It brings a lot of comfort to know they are together again.

Sheila was, of course, devastated when Mike was diagnosed with ALS and absolutely heartbroken when he passed away. She was pretty strong through it all though and very strong in general. A petite woman but one of true grit. Tiny but tough you could say, and feisty. I loved that about her. The last time I talked to her, we had a good visit. Conversation with her was always so rich. We shared how we were coping and we shared a few laughs and, like always, she told me a couple of great stories. We talked for about an hour, and then I passed the phone to Elanna. They talked for a while and I'm sure Sheila would have felt encouraged, as Elanna has a real gift of relating to, connecting with and encouraging people, especially senior folks. We signed off on a very positive note. That was Mother's Day. When I called on Father's Day, I talked to George, but Sheila was resting. My biggest regret is not writing and calling more often.

God knew all about Sheila's heartache. He knew what she suffered in her life was nothing compared to the glory He was going to reveal to her when she left this place and went to Him, and that her first day in heaven would erase the pain and heartache of everything in her life on Earth, including ALS. We can all take comfort in Romans 8:18 which says, "Yet what we suffer now is nothing compared to the glory He will reveal to us later." (NLT)

In a few weeks I'll be moving and I'm a little sad, nervous and super excited at the same time. We've been here at Elanna and Peter's house for three years and it's been awesome. I might sound like a broken record, but we couldn't have done it without them. I am so grateful for their love and support. It's time, though, for me to spread my wings and go find my way in a new place, one to call my own, and I'm taking my littlest chickadee with me.

My birthday is in a couple of days—August 5—which marks seven months from Mike's passing. Wow, time flies. I know he'd be so happy for me and my new place by the river and all the other great things happening in my life. Surely he would say to me, "Spread your wings and fly."

Sheila had a zest for life. She loved socializing and being around people. She was a lot like my own Sheila—my mom. They both had the gift of gab, they both loved to laugh, and they both told the long version of most stories.

Mike's Sheila could stay up into the wee hours of the morning, talking and reminiscing. Her stories were the best! Her Scottish accent made them even better. She did have a tendency to repeat herself, especially as she got older, which is normal. But even the same story the fifth or tenth time was just as good as the first, considering her assortment of facial expressions and comedic mannerisms, which she varied each time.

I met her after Mike and I got married. She and George came to B.C. shortly after we tied the knot to meet me and my family. The two Georges and Sheilas hit it off and I took right to my new mum-in-law. Over the years, we got closer despite the distance.

During one of our first visits, she made a comment I will never forget. She told me there was something different about me—something very special. I was so blessed by her comment and still treasure the kindness she always showed me.

During one of her solo visits a few years later, she started asking my dad a bunch of questions about his missionary work. I can still see us—Mike and I setting the table, my mom preparing food, our young children filing in for dinner and my dad praying with Sheila. She had decided to accept Jesus as her Lord and Saviour.

Over the years, we had some deep conversations. She was really smart. She had strong opinions but was open to others' ideas. She liked a good debate and questioned a lot of things (and a lot of things about God). She didn't settle for any old answer; it had to be a good answer. Sometimes, there wasn't one.

Anyway, when Mike and I prayed for her, we often prayed about her walk with the Lord. I didn't think she was connected with other Christians and sometimes wondered if she was progressing in her relationship with Jesus. One time in particular when she was really heavy on my heart, I shared with Mike that I was concerned how she might really struggle with her faith, as I knew she had doubts about different things.

Shortly after, I received a letter from her telling me she thought I might be wondering how she was doing. She told me she read her Bible fairly regularly, found comfort in its pages, and she included verses she had recently studied.

I'm sure she asked God many times, Why? *Why does my son have to endure an illness like ALS?* She probably wrestled with the Lord and begged, *Inflict me, not him.* A mother's desperate cry, I can only imagine. When she came to visit, she watched her boy handle his condition with courage and hope. She often commented about the love in our home. She complimented me and my whole family on the exceptional care we were providing for her son. Like it was not only a gift to him but (even more so) to her, his beloved mum.

I have wondered if Sheila's passing, only six months after Mike's, was ultimately the result of a broken heart. A heart now fully repaired. Questions answered. Doubts disappeared. A sealed bottle of tears.

All glory be to God!

CHAPTER 8
A Little Bird Sometimes Falls to the Earth, but God Sees Her

"So don't be afraid; you are worth more than many sparrows."
Matthew 10:31 (NIV)

Journal entry from July 13, 2011

Today, Mike and I had a really nice bike ride. Cycling has become Mike's activity of choice. He says he strangely has better balance on a bike than he does walking. We didn't go anywhere in particular, just around—down streets we haven't been before and roads we have explored many times. I enjoyed the laughter with my very best friend. It feels like we are a piece of fabric … threads woven together.

Riding bikes on the dike - Golden Ears Mountains in the background.
Six weeks post diagnosis.

Missing Mike became excruciating, but life was good. The Lord took my sorrow and gently blended the exact measure of joy into it, quite like he had done since day one of our ALS journey.

Before Mike passed away, I remember anticipating his leaving being like a ripping or tearing; like the fine threads of our glorious fabric being pulled apart. But it wasn't like that. The tapestry stayed intact. Yes, there was pain and he was gone but I learned quickly he'd always be a part of me. During this next stage, I held tightly to this: threads were protected, pain would subside, God was faithful and constant, and He would always provide.

These next blog posts are more of the same but different in ways. This is where I fear the grief gets a little mundane. But at the same time, the four or five after this next one are a few of my favourites. I hope my decision to not skip over them is the right one (I might skip one or two). I hope something in this chapter resonates with you, encourages you and others. I hope it strengthens friendships with God.

Getting Out of the Boat - Sept 11, 2015

I am so easily distracted. It's kind of crazy. I sit down to work on a blog post and end up searching "yellow lamps." I go to put on a load of laundry and find myself hanging a picture, or vice versa. Unpacking a box takes forever. Organizing my kitchen is impossible. Forget about reading a book; I can't even get through a page. I'm so forgetful, too (more than usual). I write something down so I don't forget, but I forget where I wrote it down. Sometimes I think I'm losing my mind.

I get mad at myself for being such an "airhead." I tell God I'm sorry for being so easily distracted when I'm spending time in prayer.

I've done a little research and good news; I'm not losing my mind. What I'm experiencing are symptoms of bereavement. I'm also learning that I'm pretty hard on myself and perhaps I need to cut myself some slack—everyone else is. My family and friends are so patient with me. And God, He is so patient. He loves me and He waits for me. I'm definitely learning more about His grace. Even though my prayer life isn't what is has been in the past, my communion with Him is great.

God continues to patiently direct my footsteps and He has brought me to a place I love. It's a beautiful place by the river so I think it's an appropriate time to get out of the boat. Although being at a river might make you think of getting in a boat, I'm getting out of the boat and I'm pretty sure I'm going to be okay. I'm not as afraid as I was before, although just writing that makes me burst into tears.

Most mornings since sleeping in my new bedroom, I wake up between five and five-thirty. I lie in bed and doze a little on and off until the sun rises. I watch it rise through my very large and very exceptional bedroom window. I hate to brag, but I have two of those windows in my room. One faces east, and that is of course how I can watch the sun rise—and the birds fly—and I can also look at the Fraser River and see (and hear) the trains go by. The other window faces north with a view of an empty lot and some trees. On the other side of the trees is an old historical house and museum where I have gone every day since I moved here to take Madison's new puppy, Glen, out for a walk. We play in the yard and stroll the path that leads to the next street over and a large park.

I love it here and I know Mike would love this place, too: the history, the river view, the colourful neighbourhood and all its characters. I'm constantly saying to myself and/or God and others, "Mike would love it here." Elanna says it, too.

Something is happening here in this place with the stunningly large windows, the sunrises and the river view. I think there is some healing happening here. It never occurred to me that I might need some healing but that's what I feel the Lord has in store for me here.

On another note, I really hate saying goodbye to the summer, but I gladly welcome the fall. I started my new job as an education assistant this week (on call) and continue to teach fitness classes. I'm feeling very blessed!

I really thought my summer was going to be low key, a time to unwind after a very busy and understandably tough winter and spring. I was under the impression that it was time to do nothing.

It's okay. It was a wonderful summer and here are a few of the many highlights:

I went to Victoria, B.C., twice. The first time was with my friend Karen. Her friend Jane, North Vancouver-Seymour MLA (Member of Legislative

Assembly), invited us to the Legislature. She gave an outstanding speech about ALS and the need to raise awareness and find a cure. The second time was with Nathan and Leah. We decided to go to Victoria because our trip to Toronto was postponed (until October). We had a good time visiting some of Mike's favourite places—places he and I took the kids when they were growing up—and we had a really nice visit with Mike's Aunt Aileen and cousin, Monica.

I went to Kelowna with Madison and Elanna and her family to ride in the ALS Cycle of Hope fundraiser event with Scott McComb and team. The views on that bike ride were exquisite and so are the memories made with family and friends.

Just last weekend, I climbed the beautiful Golden Ears Mountain here where we live in Maple Ridge. My children had planned on going and I thought I'd just hang back and take care of Madison's puppy. But when they mentioned taking some of Mike's ashes up to spread, I knew I had to go as well. Friends, Josh and Nuala also joined us. I had climbed the mountain once before and forgotten how grueling the trek is. Nathan has done the climb many times, but the last time the girls did it was with their dad (Nathan was along as well). As we approached the top, I became quite emotional when Erin declared, "This is where dad helped me last time." She was a little ways ahead of me, slightly out of my reach, and I wished I could have just extended my hand and placed it on her to make her feel secure like her dad did. Mike would be so proud of Erin climbing that mountain just a year after her hip replacement surgery. He was so proud of his children and would have been thrilled that they climbed the mountain he loved in honour and memory of him.

As excited as I am about my new home, I miss the one we left. Elanna, Peter, Michaela and Luke made their home ours. I know it's hard for Elanna, in particular; first, Mike left, and she and he were very close. They were great friends for many years and like blood brother and sister. She tells me often how much she misses him. And now Madison and I are gone, so there will be an even bigger void. But Elanna and I will always be really close; whether living apart or in the same house. We are more than sisters; we are best friends.

Elanna and Peter can't possibly know how much it meant to us to stay in their home. They thought it was perfect. At first we said no; we didn't want to impose. We quickly saw the bigger picture, though, and agreed it was a good idea. Elanna, to this day, says how grateful she is to have that house—with ground-level entry and suite, beautiful guest bedroom and just enough bathroom space to accommodate Mike's commode. She, Peter and the kids have hosted other family and friends over the years and even family of friends they didn't know. They are more than happy to share their lovely home. Elanna still says she can't believe she had doubts about it when they were looking to purchase and how God knew all along His grand plans for it. She also reminded me lately how when they moved in, they went from room to room committing each one to God and asking Him to use their new house for His glory.

Michaela, Elanna, Peter and Luke on their front porch
- always a warm welcome.

I can't imagine me and Mike getting by as well in any other situation. I've called it a "special time" in our lives before, but it was extraordinary. I am still over at Elanna and Peter's house quite often to visit, especially since our mom passed away. We gather there with my dad a lot. It still feels like home to me.

I will always treasure the memories of family gatherings there and my mom giving Mike head rubs and cutting his hair. Other memories include: our kids and Leah and my parents coming and going, watching Michaela and Luke growing and observing such kindness in their hearts; Mike's mum's and his sister's frequent visits, Elanna and Peter's immediate assistance when needed, anyone and everyone hanging out by the pool, watching TV with whoever wanted to join us, neighbours and friends dropping food off now and then, Mike's favourite flowers in the backyard and, recently, his memorial tree planted in the front; the list goes on. I'm so glad and so grateful this was God's plan from the start. What an exceptional experience to spend our last few years together in that extraordinary place where people and God's love congregate.

Spreading my wings and flying away from that house was exhilarating, and at the same time somewhat devastating. Elanna and I became unbelievably close; I grew very attached to all four of them. But off I went like a little bird to my own nest (Madison came along). I got a mortgage by myself and started paying bills again and stood on my own. This is also where God got me alone and reminded me of the word He gave me at the beginning of a treacherous ALS journey...

Conversations with the Man I Love - Sept 21, 2015

Half-dressed after getting out of the bath with a towel on my head, I lie across my bed and stare at the great outdoors through my window—the river and the trees and some buildings in the distance. I feel totally exposed, not that anyone can see me, but exposed as I lay myself bare before the Lord. I'm trying to just "be" so He can do a work in me, but that's not easy. My high expectations say, get up, clean up, make your bed, get going, but I'm trying to be still. I feel I'm supposed to learn the discipline of "Don't just do something, stand there." Instead of what comes more naturally; "Don't just stand there, do something."

If you read my last blog post, you will know that I've figured out some of what God has in store for me in this place, and that is *healing*. It totally took me by surprise because I didn't think I needed any "healing." I'm really okay, but I guess God's not okay with just "okay" ... I guess He wants more than that for me.

So, with the revelation of "healing" I'm trying to not dodge what God is doing. I kind of feel like I'm back in elementary school in line for a vaccination shot or something. It's scary and uncomfortable and I want to run in the other direction, but I'm not running. I'm actually trying to be still, which is hard most of the time. It's like, how can I be still when I've got bills to pay, a dog to walk, a floor to mop, dishes to wash, shopping to do and a workout to get to?

There needs to be stillness physically, but I'm learning a stillness in spirit is just as—or more—important. So even when I'm doing those things, my spirit and mind are "still" and available to Him and His working, His healing, His comforting, His loving, His directing. It's about making me available to go with Him where He wants me to go even though it really hurts. And even though I say, "go with Him," it might be more about "staying with Him." I might have to "move" through something but "stay put" in Him.

Part of what I'm learning is to stop squirming when certain thoughts and memories come to mind, like thoughts of Mike's touch. It's a painful place to go, but a very wonderful place, too. That place I once knew, tightly wrapped in his loving arms. The feeling of goose bumps when he swept my hair off my neck and put his lips there or same when he'd draw a slow soft line down my bare spine with the back of a few fingers.

ALS took Mike's touch away from me a few years ago already, along with the sound of his voice and the ease of conversation. Fresher memories are those of one-letter-at-a-time conversations that challenged, but also strengthened our patience and love. The scent of peppermint body wash and Old Spice deodorant linger, along with the sound of his breathing, and his few looks that conveyed many things. My lover, my caregiver, my encourager, my adviser, my helper, my friend all in one … my beloved companion! I miss him as my "companion" the most. Companions come and go in this life, but there is one Companion who never leaves.

Only a few weeks after Mike was diagnosed with ALS, my friend Celeste asked me if I would join her at her church for a ladies' meeting. The meeting was about prayer mentors and Celeste invited me to come as her guest, as her prayer mentor. I was honoured, of course, not only to be considered her prayer mentor but to stand with her and share.

When I prayed about what I should say that day to a room full of women who were looking for some prayer wisdom and inspiration, I got this word: "companion." It was the most excellent word I could have heard at the beginning of a treacherous journey with ALS. At the beginning of a journey of letting go of my husband and best friend, Jesus said, "Here I am, your greatest and forever companion." I didn't share with the women there that day that my beloved husband had just been diagnosed with a terminal illness, but I did share from my heart about my greatest, highest and forever Companion and about my conversations with this Man I love. Conversations I call "prayer," a closeness I can't compare; a relationship with the Almighty—my Lord, Saviour and Friend and forever Companion—Jesus!

I just love the old hymn written in 1855 about friendship with the Lord by Joseph M. Scriven titled "What a friend we have in Jesus." He reminds us that Jesus bears our grief and sin, and that through prayer it's a privilege to give everything to Him. He questions if we can find a friend as faithful, one who shares all our sorrows. Because He knows our weaknesses and our despair, we should take everything to the Lord in prayer!

He was there somewhere before, gently wooing me, and then He was right here. I believed in Him; I knew a little bit about Him from my studies in Catechism, but He became a part of me when I asked Him to come into my heart as a young teen. When I accepted Him and opened the door of my life to Him and acknowledged Him as Lord and Saviour, He became my Friend. I compare our relationship to the most exquisite garden. A garden that continues to grow and has become lush and colourful over all these years. He took a dry patch of land and gave it Life. He gave me Life. He is the Life!

The Bible says He is the Way, the Truth and the Life. He is the Bread of Life and the Living Water; a Hiding Place, a Friend of sinners.

Best friends are to be treasured indeed, but of course no one compares to Him. He is the Good Shepherd; Protector, Healer, Restorer, Redeemer. He is the Light of the world; the epitome of love. He is Jesus!

Sometimes, just hearing His name, or saying it, emits emotions in me I can't explain. It's the most beautiful name!

Nathan preaches at a couple of different local churches sometimes to relieve pastors when sick or on holidays, etc. A recent sermon was about truth. What is it and how to find it. Of course, it's ultimately Jesus. Nathan's message was thought-provoking, like always, and simple yet profound—a statement he's heard from me before about his sermons.

Anyway, at the end he talked about the name of Jesus. He said His name in Hebrew and mentioned different pronunciations. Then he asked if His name was that much more special than the average name. He questioned why we think it's so beautiful. My first thought was that His name could be anything and it would be beautiful because of who He is. "Jesus" is a nice name, but it's so beautiful because of the person He is, the Lord, Saviour and Friend He is to me. Nathan pretty much echoed my thoughts and by the nodding of heads, I'd say everyone agreed.

Nathan ended with something like this: "When we profess the name of Jesus, we are professing Him, who He is and was. We are professing the Truth. There is power in His name."

"And being found in human form, He humbled Himself by becoming obedient to the point of death, even death on a cross. Therefore, God has highly exalted Him and bestowed on Him the name that is above every name, so that at the name of Jesus every knee should bow, in heaven and on earth and under the earth, and every tongue confess that Jesus Christ is Lord, to the glory of God the Father."

Philippians 2:8-11 (ESV)

A Little Bird and a Can of Worms - Oct 7, 2015

While on our hike up the Golden Ears Mountain last month, an injured (or sick) bird fell right in front of us. The bird maybe fell out of a tree or rolled down the mountain, we weren't sure, but the poor thing fell right in front of us. Her eyes were open but she wasn't moving. I felt bad for Nathan, who made sure the beautiful creature was in fact dead and not suffering. I felt bad for the little bird, for the bird's mother, brother or whoever. I let the others get ahead a few steps and I cried and hiked and cried. The death of this bird opened up a can of worms for me. I prayed for Nathan, that the image of the dead bird wouldn't stay with him (just like I've prayed the image of his dead father wouldn't stay with him and his sisters). And I prayed for all of us who have experienced the inevitable heartbreak of death ... which would be almost all of us, if not all of us.

It was just a bird, I thought, *Why am I so upset?* But it wasn't just a bird; it was a lovely living, breathing thing and then it was dead ... no breath. Nathan consoled me by telling me that the bird was probably long gone by the time we came along. It helped a little. Still, I grieved and hiked and grieved.

Death is all around us. I don't want to sound like a downer, but it's true. Death is all around us, and it's part of life. It's funny how we never get used to it even though it's inevitable.

The other day, I listened to Mike's and my playlist for the first time since we parted. It's the playlist we listened to throughout the night before he passed and during his last breaths while I sang to him and said goodbye. Right away, I was back in that room by his bedside. Those of us in the room at the time watched the pulse in his neck, wondering if it really was going to stop like the nurse said it would. We still didn't believe it was going to stop until it did, and then we wondered which one was the last, as if we could go back and catch that last one and hold onto it forever. I remember feeling the life in that room even though death had just occurred; I could barely breathe. There was more life in that room than death. It was a room of life—a good room, even though it was a room of sorrow and grief.

I went to three memorial services last week, speaking of grief. One was for the grandma of a young friend. One was for my Auntie Marlene's daughter (Auntie Marlene is my mom's first cousin). She lost one daughter a number of years ago, and this daughter she lost suddenly a few weeks ago (and she lost her husband some time in between). As I was choking out the words, "I'm so terribly sorry..." Auntie Marlene said to me, "You have had such a tremendous loss." I tearfully replied something like, "I can't imagine your loss—this loss of a second daughter." She looked around for her son and sadly and happily stated, "Both my girls are gone ... but I still have Brad."

The third memorial service, which was actually the first of the three, was for five people and it was at Elanna's place of work (a long-term care facility). Elanna leads memorial services there every few months for the residents who have passed away. Sometimes I wonder how Elanna does it. She cares for and loves these people (she works in recreation, but they call her "nurse" and she fills both roles well). She builds relationships with them and gets to know their families, and then eventually she has to say goodbye. It's a lot of "goodbyes" over the course of a career.

I didn't know any of the people being remembered and honoured at this memorial service, but I know the son and daughter-in-law of one of the women—good friends of my Auntie Marguerite.

The memorial service for five was lovely. The music was so nice and the short glimpses into each of their lives was interesting. Pictures got passed around and the stories shared by some of the family members were touching. Elanna and a co-worker did an excellent job of leading the service. The room had a very peaceful glow and there was comfort there ... of course some sorrow, but peace and comfort. It opened another can of worms for me.

That night, Elanna, Michaela and I went to see the movie *The Intern* starring Anne Hathaway and Robert

De Niro. It's not a sad movie, but it was a tearjerker for me and Elanna. At one point, Michaela (fifteen years old) looked at her mom and questioned, "Are you crying?" Then she turned to me to tell me her mom was crying (as if that was pretty funny) and saw me crying. "Are you crying, too, Auntie?" she asked.

Robert De Niro's character, Ben, captured our hearts—a seventy-year-old retired widower who looks for a useful way to spend his time, applies for a senior intern position at an online fashion company, and gets the job.

Ben comes from a world where chivalry is alive and well. He explains to a young fellow intern that men carry handkerchiefs because women cry. It's like he understands the depths of a woman: her sensitivity and her amazing strength, and he just supports it. He understands the value of making a difference and being a part of someone else's "difference." He actually reminded me quite a bit of my dad. And as Michaela pointed out a few times, there is a resemblance between the two in some scenes.

While Robert De Niro was capturing my heart, so was an older couple two rows ahead of us. During the coming attractions, I happened to catch a glimpse of the two lovebirds holding hands. It wasn't your typical handholding, though; it was the exact way Mike held my hand every time we went to the movies. He would take my hand in his and pull it over onto his lap and rub slow, gentle circles and other patterns on the back of it. He frequently lifted it up to his mouth and kissed it. I didn't notice this "smooth operator" do any kissing, but every ten minutes or so, when I leaned toward Michaela and took a look between the couple right in front of us, I saw the man rubbing his sweetheart's hand ... he didn't stop. When he got up to go to the washroom (or wherever), he was definitely an elderly man. He used the hand railing and slowly and carefully went down the stairs. I thought to myself, *That was going to be us.*

You might be wondering where I'm going with this "A Little Bird and a Can of Worms" story, and quite frankly, I'm wondering where I'm going with it as well. Perhaps it's just a reminder to savour every moment, to give thanks in all circumstance and to cherish the love. Keep breathing, keep giving and keep going. Don't take anything for granted, be hopeful, forgive the way you want to be forgiven, and trust in the Lord with all your heart.

Death is part of life and the gateway to heaven for those who put their faith in Jesus; and the best is yet to come!

I'm heading to Toronto tomorrow morning to visit family and see Mike's memorial tree and spread some of his and his mum's ashes near Highland Creek where Mike grew up. It's going to be a very blessed Thanksgiving, and I'm sure there will be another can of worms there waiting for me.

"Are not two small birds sold for a very small piece of money? And yet not one of the birds falls to the earth without your Father knowing it."
Matthew 10:29 (NLT)

Madison, me, Nathan and Erin on our way up the Golden Ears Mountains in our hometown of Maple Ridge, B.C.

"Like a bird protecting its young, God will cover you with His feathers, will protect you under His great wings; His faithfulness will form a shield around you, a rock-solid wall to protect you."
Psalm 91:4 (The Voice)

CHAPTER 9
God's Sovereignty and the Importance of Fresh Breath

"We can make our plans, but the Lord determines our steps."
Proverbs 16:9 (NLT)

The dictionary describes "sovereign" with words like supreme authority, dominion, ruler, royalty. When I think of the Father's sovereignty, I think of those things, but more personally, I think of how He has me in the palm of His hand; how He is present when I fall asleep at night and right there in the morning when I wake up again.

He's all-powerful, all-knowing, all-loving and He's in complete control. It's a difficult concept sometimes, considering the world seems to be completely out of control. A common question asks, *How can a loving God allow so much pain, suffering and chaos?* Some answers talk about human freewill and this fallen world's brokenness. But who am I to even try to answer? All I can say is that Mike and I had long committed our lives to Christ, and we stayed as close to Him as we possibly could, and there was peace that surpassed all understanding. There was peace in the middle of our storm, hope—an anchor for our souls; His love like teeming rain, lavishly poured.

Journal entry from July 13, 2011

For the last few weeks when Mike and I go to bed, I ask Mike to use words to describe how he feels about his illness, and then we pray about those feelings (an exercise we've been doing from the book we have been reading called *The Healing Code*). He started with words like anxious, worried, scared, sad and helpless. Over time it became, "a little anxious, a little sad, a little worried." Tonight when I inquired, he replied, "Content."

Journal entry from July 14, 2011

Tonight when I asked Mike to describe how he felt about his illness, he responded, "Resolved." He's at peace.

~

We Had Christmas - Dec 13, 2015

I'm not really the "feeling sorry for myself" type, but recently I was a little tempted. Thankfully, it only lasted for a few seconds. I was walking home from the Rec Centre where I teach fitness classes, enjoying the evening and minding my own business, when all of a sudden I remembered it's my first Christmas apart from Mike. It was like, *Oh yeah, this is my first Christmas without him (I should be really sad).* But sadness didn't have a chance to enter in because this was my next thought, *It's Mike's first Christmas in heaven!* Whomp, abundant joy. For a minute there, I was walking on air. I felt like dancing.

A few people have expressed some concern for me as we approach Christmas, it being my first Christmas apart from Mike. While I really appreciate the care and concern of family and friends, I honestly think I'm going to be all right. This is what I have to say: "We had Christmas."

I'll never forget the man I met a few days before my book signing at Save-On-Foods back in April when my book first launched. I was there to meet with my friend Shelley, who invited me to do the book signing. She and I were going over the details of the event when a customer she knew well came over to her to say hello. She introduced us and told him about my book. He was a friendly and jokey guy, but as soon as he heard my book was about my husband who had ALS, his smile disappeared. He shared that his wife also had ALS. He told us she passed away years ago and proceeded to draw us a picture of their experience. Understandably, he was still very hurt. Unfortunately, he was bitter and angry. It wasn't a pretty picture. ALS, of course, isn't pretty, but this man and his family had experienced complete devastation. There was no indication of peace or joy … just lost hope and grief.

While comparing stories, this man told me his wife passed away just before Christmas. The last thing he said to me when he left the grocery store was, "You had Christmas." I replied gratefully, "Yes, we had Christmas."

We had many wonderful Christmases and last Christmas was extra special. I knew in my heart it was our last one together, and I'm sure Mike knew it as well. We cherished every minute of it. This year, Mike spends Christmas in heaven and I am overjoyed for him!

We had Christmas, so please don't be sad for me. Yes, there will be tears over the next few weeks (more than usual probably), but the joy outweighs the grief (like most of the time)

Our first Christmas without Mike
- sorrowful and joyful at the same time.

Lips Are For Kissing - Dec 30, 2015

I have almost forgotten what a kiss on the lips feels like. Once in a while, Leah gives me a kiss on the lips. It's so sweet because I usually turn my head so she can plant one on my cheek, but she follows my lips with her pucker, and I get the softest, sweetest kiss right on the lips.

On Christmas day, my two-and-a-half-year-old great-nephew Xavier planted a couple on me, and I was like, *Oh yeah, LIPS ... they are for kissing.*

It's kind of weird when you think about it—kissing, that is. It's weird, but it's absolutely wonderful as well. It's been a while for me (I'm talking the romantic kind of kiss now) and with New Year's Eve approaching,

I'm thinking about it more and more. Plus, I'm a real sucker (no pun intended) for all those made-for-TV Christmas romance movies and for the classics too, all of which I've watched over the last couple of weeks.

Anyway, at some point during Mike's battle with ALS he lost the ability to kiss, so it's been about three years since I've had a good one. I wish I could remember the last really good kiss—the last full lip-lock, total embrace, when his lips reached out for mine and vice versa. I guess it doesn't matter. What matters is we had lots of them. So my advice to anyone interested in my advice: kiss! Kiss a lot. Really plant one on him (or her) … and let your lips linger.

Happy New Year!

It's funny because that first New Year's was harder for me than Christmas. I think because it's so romanticized on TV and in movies: the dancing, the countdown, the kiss. But for most people, is it really like this? It wasn't for me and Mike. We always had a kiss at the stroke of midnight, but the evening was usually low key. Some New Year's Eves were spent with friends, and all the later ones with family.

That "not so special" stroke-of-midnight kiss obviously meant more to me than I realized. We were never at a dinner and dance or fireworks display, but it was romantic in a Mike and Nadine kind of way. I didn't think much of it, but it wasn't just a kiss, I guess; it was a *Hey, here we are another year and I love you even more than the one before* kind of moment. We talked about doing something more romantic some future New Year's when the kids were all grown up. We never did, but that's okay. I'll take what we had over "something more special" any day.

After our traditional family dinner out that first New Year's without Mike, I stood alone on the balcony at midnight. I missed my beloved more than ever, dreaming about our stroke-of-midnight kiss, and there in the distance: fireworks!

Chasing a Rainbow - Jan 16, 2016

I set one goal last New Year, and that was to keep Mike alive for as long as I possibly could. He died five days later. I guess you could say I failed that one miserably … not really. Sometimes God's plans get in the way of our plans, and whether we like it or not His are always better than ours. Sometimes I agonize over the fact that I could have done more, but God is so much bigger than I am and greater than anything I could or couldn't do for Mike. He took Mike in His perfect timing. Case closed.

On January 5th we celebrated Mike's first anniversary in heaven. I use the word "celebrate" loosely. I booked the day off and Elanna had the day off, so we went to Fort Langley (we would have invited our mom, but it was pouring). There were other places we thought of going, places Mike liked, but I couldn't get the Fort Langley cemetery off my mind. Mike loved it there. He loved cemeteries. It must have been the history buff in him. He liked walking around and reading the headstones … the names and dates. He guessed the type of life the particular person lived and that sort of thing.

It was raining, so Elanna and I didn't go around reading headstones, but we enjoyed our time there reminiscing about Mike with a few tears and lots of laughs. We spread some of Mike's ashes in the area, mostly around big lovely trees. We also browsed in the shops and had lunch at Wendel's Bookstore and Cafe. Mike would have been very pleased. We sat at our favourite seat by the window where we sat with him and our mom the last time we were there together.

After Mike died I tried to not make plans, set goals or dream dreams. At times I wanted to forge a path and plow ahead but, as difficult as it was, I resisted—most of the time. Like I wrote in my post "Conversations With the Man I Love," I feel like I'm supposed to learn the discipline of "Don't just do something, stand there." There was healing in not filling my life with "things to do." The only thing on my "list of things to do" was to rest in the palm of His hand and trust Him on a deeper level.

In the evening of the 5th, I took Erin up on her offer to teach my Pilates class and I went for a long walk. I didn't think about where I was going; I just went. It wasn't late, but it was dark. I live in a "sketchy" area of town, but I never feel nervous there. About an hour into my walk, I found myself on a street that does make me feel a little nervous. After being startled by someone (totally innocently), I picked up my pace and took the first right down a road better lit. I ended up behind someone smoking, so jogging,

I crossed over and stopped abruptly right where my foot landed on the sidewalk on the other side.

The little Christmas lights in the window of the store I now stood in front of got my attention, along with the paper Canadian flags that hung across the top. The books, which were lined up in rows almost pressing against the crystal clear glass, drew me closer. "Ken's Bookcase" appeared in sticky letters smack dab in the middle of it all, and I still didn't get it. God was speaking to me, but it took me a few minutes before I heard Him. I had passed by this little used bookstore a few times before and had been inside once many years ago. I had gone in to check out the Bibles. I was interested in having a different version to compare with my New International Version (before I used the internet to do that sort of thing). I still remember that hardcover-with-jacket gem on a high shelf squished in between others less brilliant-looking. It was a Woman's Study Bible, practically new. I pulled it down and examined the weight of it, the scent of it, the sheer genius of it. Then I opened it and a sunbeam or something like that shone from it. I recognized the handwriting of the inscription on the front page immediately. It was the writing of my friend Colleen.

I wrote about Colleen and her husband Chris in my book *Hold On, Let Go*. Colleen and Chris were our business partners for five years. We owned and operated Fitness Works together, a fitness studio from 1994-1999. In my book, I describe these two as a little older than us and very wise—spiritual mentors. This is what I say about Colleen in Chapter Ten: *Colleen has a really good sense of timing. She listens to that little voice in her, prompting her to call or send a message. When she phones me early in the morning and suggests we pray for my parents who are out on the mission field, I don't ask why she is calling so early or let her know she woke me up, I just agree.*

Colleen was always up and still is up to the Lord's business, so finding this Bible she gave to a young friend (who I also knew) was not a surprise.

I actually kept the Bible for a little while and beautified my own bookcase with it, exploring it on and off. I wasn't seeing Colleen on a regular basis at the time (this was shortly after we closed our business) and kept forgetting to give it to her. I eventually took it to her and told her the story. Regardless of that, and how the book got in the store and why, I don't doubt for one minute that the Lord directed my steps to that little bookstore that glowed in the dark on my walk the other night. God wanted to remind me that nothing gets by Him. That He is the orchestrator of the universe and that He placed the stars in the sky and named them; He covered seashores with tiny grains of sand. It's nothing for Him to get a book back in the rightful owner's hands or cure a dying man ... according to His plan, it will be, or not.

When the new year was fast approaching, I did what I felt I should; I started setting goals, planning and dreaming. You know, like a "New Year, New You" idea. But then I said in my head, *Hey, this you is okay. This you is on the right track.* Plus, when I look back on last year—the year of one goal that failed miserably—more happened than I could ever imagine. I finished a college program, graduated and started a new career. I became an author, a speaker and a spokesperson for ALS. I moved into a beautiful new home by the river with a spectacular view—a dream (I didn't really dream) come true. I went places, met people and did things I couldn't have planned had I tried. These were God's plans, not mine.

So, this New Year's, I'm only setting one goal again. I know I have things I need to improve upon in my life and I've made a mental note of them, but the only goal I'm writing down this New Year's, the only one I'm setting in stone, is to stay as close to Him as I possibly can, to stay put in the palm of His hand and with my whole heart keep trusting Him. (Okay, so it has three parts).

On the 6th of January (the day after Mike's anniversary), I got up early like I do most mornings and got ready for work in case I got called in. I figured if I didn't get called in, I'd go to my friend Keri's fitness class at 8:50 a.m. When I didn't get a call and had some time to spare, I sat in front of my living room window and watched the sun come up. I thought about the day before and contemplated God's faithfulness and His mercies that are new every morning. As the sun burst forth, so did joy in my heart. I praised Him for a while before I noticed the lightest drops of rain floating through the air. This is when I "burst forth" and scrambled to get my things together, knowing a rainbow would be out there somewhere. I grabbed everything I needed for the class and ran up to the roof of my building to see about a rainbow. Sure enough, there is was, on the other side of my building … it was beautiful. The other half of the rainbow was in full view at the end of my street that I walked up to go to Keri's class at the Rec Centre. I kept zigzagging across the street to see it from the best angle.

I apologized as I ran into class a little late. Keri and I both asked at the same time, "Did you see the rainbow?" The class was fantastic as always, and again at the end I mentioned I was sorry for being late and added, "But I was chasing a rainbow." Keri suggested, "There's your next blog post title." I told her I was thinking the same thing.

Rainbows are a good reminder of God's promises, His unconditional love and faithfulness, His justice, His Sovereignty.

Mike's birthday is today, January 16th. We have now experienced all the "firsts." You see them coming and don't want them to come, but want them to be behind you at the same time. They are all behind us now, but I can't say that makes it any easier. We are blessed to be doing quite well, nonetheless. Thanks again for your support and prayers.

"The Lord directs our steps, so why try to understand everything along the way?"
Proverbs 20:24 (NLT)

Do we truly believe God is good? Oh sure, He is good when life is going well, but what about in hard times and during trials? When we lose someone we dearly love and grief and sorrow strike, do we retract our belief that God is good, or do we trust He's good all the time? Comfort and hope come from knowing God is in control, even when something makes no sense at all. His ways are higher than our ways.

"God's love is meteoric, His loyalty astronomic, His purpose titanic, His verdict oceanic. Yet in His largeness nothing gets lost; not a man, not a mouse, slips through the cracks."
Psalm 36:5-6 (Message)

CHAPTER 10
Dark Clouds, Lemon Drops and Diamonds in the Rough

"Oh, how sweet the light of day, and how wonderful to live in the sunshine! Even if you live a long time, don't take a single day for granted. Take delight in each light-filled hour, remembering that there will also be many dark days..."

Ecclesiastes 11:7 (Message)

Journal entry from March 6, 2011

I had a dream last night. Mike and I were on the side of a road, about to cross it, when an earthquake happened. There were other people with us, just behind us; I think it was family and other people we knew. We held them back until the earthquake passed. I was so relieved we were all okay when it stopped. The road was destroyed though; it was broken. There were huge cracks and crevices. But the bumps in the road seemed like nothing because we were unharmed.

~

That second journal entry from the day before Mike's ALS diagnosis is a reminder of the internal storm that was going on inside me. We suspected ALS and had been waiting as patiently as we could for Mike's appointment with the neurologist in hopes of hearing we were wrong. That dream is also a reminder of the peace. The eternal peace that is in me because of the Holy Spirit, is immeasurably stronger than any storm.

Journal entry from January 19, 2014

It's like a downward spiral when I take my eyes off the Lord - when I dwell on difficulties. "Help me to keep my eyes on you, God." Let nothing come between us, I tell myself.

~

A Dark Cloud and a Silver Lining - Mar 18, 2016

I've been resisting writing this one for a while. I haven't been eager to talk about it, but I'll just say it right out: there has been a dark cloud, mostly throughout January and February (although, it's still kind of hanging around). Your first thought probably is that I live in the Greater Vancouver area so, of course, there has been a dark cloud; there have been many, many dark clouds. The fact that it is grey and rainy a lot here during this time of year doesn't help, but if you haven't guessed yet, I'm talking figuratively about a dark cloud. You know, one of those heavy, low-lying kind that follows you (only you) around all the time.

Throughout January, I prepared to tell Mike's and my story to a group of clinical counsellors at an information and recruitment meeting for the ALS Society of B.C. The ALS Society provides free counselling to anyone affected by ALS, so they rely on counsellors to volunteer their time. Executive Director and friend Wendy told me later that day that it was a very successful meeting; they had more people sign up to do this good work than ever before. I was so pleased to hear that, but preparing for and presenting that day was very emotional for me. I read some blog posts to the group and really emphasized Mike's positive attitude and strong faith while trying to give them a realistic glimpse into the cruel world of ALS. It was weighty for sure, but like I've told Wendy a few times, "However I can help, whatever I can do for you and the ALS Society, please just let me know."

It's a similar conversation I've had with my friend Darryl, who has ALS. He sent me a message recently with a beautiful picture he had taken. I asked him how he was doing. This was his reply: "I almost wrote you earlier in the week—Sunday and Monday were bad days—but then decided against it. It might be too painful to talk about ALS specifics."

My reply: "Please feel free to message me anytime, day or night. ALS is so painful, but I'm in for life. The good Lord provided the support, love and help we needed when we needed it, and I want to be there for others."

The presentation for the ALS Society was just one thing, but there were other contributing factors in the heavy mixed emotions of my dark cloud. I'm not sure if I can pinpoint them all, but these are probably some: grief, a little bit of regret, doubt, some sadness, anxiety, fear and worry. "Fear" and "worry" always lead to guilt, especially considering I've been shouting from the rooftops that "I'm trusting in the Lord with all my heart!" Well, from my rooftop anyway, and from a number of blog posts over the last few months. "Trusting the Lord" is something I've emphasized in all my writing and recently in my speech for the Apologetics Canada "Thinking" Conference I spoke at on March 5th.

Under this dark cloud of heaviness, I really felt God encouraging me to stay there. I think I heard Him say, "Don't run." I wanted to run. Like other times, I just wanted to escape, and quickly, but this time more than any other time, I felt like I was supposed to embrace all those "ugly" feelings and find God in that mucky place.

It's a bit of a battle zone there, though. Can anyone else hear the negative voices? You might think I'm really losing it now or you might be a little relieved that you aren't the only one who hears them. A few of mine sound like this: "You can't do this on your own," and "You are going to fail," and "God has rescued you every time, but this time He might just want to teach you a lesson," and "You can trust Him, but you should still be afraid," and "You aren't worthy of God's love or anyone else's." It's all lies, of course, so why do I entertain them?

Leading up to the Thinking Conference, I heard these lies: "This is a mistake. No one wants to hear what you have to say. Who cares, anyway?" And "You are such a fraud, such a loser, such a fake ..." Ironically, my speech title was "Worrier to Warrior."

The dark cloud along with all those icky feelings is one thing, but the voices are like a torrential downpour, like a pelting of fiery darts ... at night in the dark, all alone. Oh, my goodness, where is He? And then you start feeling around for God and calling out to Him.

He says, "Be still and know that I am God." Not, be still and feel that I am God. Thankfully He is there; so much relief. But the fear doesn't necessarily disappear.

Sometimes it feels like He's not there at all. Like I heard in a recent sermon by Pastor Bradley, the Psalmist cries out to God "Where are you?" And even in that despair, there is hope. We have to ask Him where He is ... has He forgotten me? But just by asking, we know He is there even though we don't see, feel, or hear Him. We just know.

Ultimately, He is there. And that is where my trust proves stronger than the negative voices. That is where hope and even joy is stronger, and I can't be separated from those things or His extravagant love. Nothing can separate us from His love!

God gave us an array of feelings, and for some reason most of us only want to feel happy; we resist sadness and any other emotions that don't make us "feel good." But here is the silver lining: we really get to know God in those dark places—the sad, scary places. I guess we could shrivel up and die there, but if we trust in the Lord there, we will more likely grow there. We have a tendency to call out to Him there, we get to know Him better ... and that's the silver lining!

I certainly don't invite sorrow, but I'm trying to learn from Mike. He taught me something extremely valuable that I will never forget. Shortly after he was diagnosed, he thanked God for the things he wanted in his life and the things he didn't want, like ALS. He said that ALS would teach him to fully rely on God. So like a good student, I'm giving thanks for the things I want in my life and the things I don't want, like grief, struggle and strife.

"The discipline of dismay is an essential lesson which a disciple must learn. But when the darkness of dismay comes, endure until it is over, because out of it will come the ability to follow Jesus truly, which brings inexpressibly wonderful joy."
Oswald Chambers

Spring officially starts on Sunday and we've been experiencing more sunshine and blue skies, but regardless of the weather outside I can feel the dark cloud lifting from me. I wish I could say I've enjoyed my time under the dark cloud, but not really, although I have drawn closer to the Lord and that is always a good thing.

I'm just going to finish with this encouraging story. You know those negative voices I told you I was hearing before the conference? Well, the night before the conference I received a Facebook message from someone I didn't know, and through it God showed up in His usual perfect timing to help me battle the lies.

It started like this:

"My name is Chris Ryan and I wanted to write to you to share my experience over the last year. My beautiful wife, Heather, passed away from cancer on August 14, 2015. In June 2014 we found out that the cancer had metastasized to her brain and formed eight tumours. She was given only months to live..."

Chris continued to tell about his wife's determination to prove her oncologist wrong and how, after she battled long and hard, when there was nothing more doctors could do for her, she and Chris decided to make wonderful memories together and live life to the fullest.

Chris went on to tell me how he found my book at the House of James Bookstore in Abbotsford where they lived; he said it looked like a book that could help him. It took him a while to find the courage to pick it up and actually read it. It wasn't until a few months after Heather passed away that he did.

He continued:

"I could relate to your story. Watching your spouse slowly fade away right in front of you can be difficult; however, it can also be beautiful if your faith in God is strong enough. The combination of your writing, Michael's writing, the mixture of Scripture and the words of Oswald Chambers strengthened my resolve to not let my loss take over me.

"I have started following your blog and your writings continue to bring me joy and comfort. Here's one example: after reading your blog post "We had Christmas," I had one of the best Christmases ever. I became excited for Heather as it was her first Christmas in Heaven (as well as my Dad's—he passed two months before her). That thought brought me so much happiness and peace and I wouldn't have thought about it that way if I hadn't read your post.

"I want to say thank you! Because of your insight,

I have been able to look at things in a more positive light. I am a better person today because of Heather's love and God's love and I feel complete joy in my life."

Heather and Chris

I replied to Chris and thanked him for his timely words of encouragement. We started communicating and a beautiful friendship quickly emerged.

One day during this time, my friend Adele pulled me aside after a spin class. It's not unusual for us to chat after class, but this day she clearly had something heavy on her heart to say. She told me that at her age, if she lost her beloved husband she'd be too old for another one. She said she'd be okay— she has her pickle ball, hip hop dance classes and group fitness. She proceeded, "But you're young. You should open your heart to another love."

Over the next few weeks, Adele reiterated her speech. When I told her about my new friendship with Chris and how he had asked me out for coffee but I hadn't replied yet, she said, "It's just coffee. Don't be afraid. Go get your feet wet."

Good Men Empower Women - April 1, 2016

For the last few months, I've been alternating my wedding band from my left hand to my right hand. I'll put it on my right hand for a while and forget about it, and then without thinking I'll slip it back on my left ring finger and eventually notice it's there. It's definitely the most comfortable there. It fits nicely into the groove that has been worn into that finger for twenty-seven years. There's an indentation there that I thought would never disappear, but it's slowly fading as the ring spends more time on the right side.

When Mike and I picked out my first engagement ring and wedding band, we weren't preparing for a long engagement filled with elaborate wedding plans. We were getting ready to board a flight to Los Angeles for an elopement … a "shotgun wedding." It was a quick decision and the rings were just a necessity. We were young and had a small budget, so I just settled for a nice set—not my dream engagement ring.

On our tenth wedding anniversary, I decided I had outgrown the set, not physically, but I was older and my little diamond looked slightly out of place on my more mature finger. I didn't pine for a bigger diamond; I told Mike I didn't need a diamond at all. We put the "two months' salary" (or whatever the jewelry store commercials suggest you spend) towards bills and groceries like always, and I just got a band. A lovely gold band, simple and pretty with a faint swirly design etched on it.

At twenty-plus years of marriage, I was wearing more silver jewelry and was casually looking for a silver, or preferably, a white gold ring. I wanted something with a heart on it (I've got a thing for hearts). Sure enough, at one of those kiosks while at the Toronto airport (after spending time there with Mike's family) on our travels to Bulgaria for Mike's stem cell treatment, I found exactly what I had in mind at the cost of $18.99, and I've been wearing it with pride ever since.

Just before Christmas, I taught a type of fitness class I had never taught before, a Barre class (pronounced "bar"). It's a blend of Pilates, ballet and strength moves. I've had the Pilates and strength moves down pat for years, but the ballet was something new. I attended a workshop and a few classes before I taught Barre and I fell in love with it right away.

During that first class I attended, there was a moment in particular that caught me off-guard and had nothing to do with grand plies or arabesques. When the instructor asked us to position ourselves in front of the mirror and to place our hands on the bar, I lost sight of everything except the assembly line of diamond rings. Every left hand on that bar had a glow; not everyone was a diamond, but every ring finger was taken. It was like a special wives' club meeting at the bar … the ballet bar, that is, and I felt like an imposter.

I watched in slow-motion-like every time all the lovely hands returned to the bar. All those hardworking, hard-loving, wonderful, wife hands coming together into place to give thanks, to praise, to escape, to run away or whatever, at the end of a long day.

There were definitely times over the years that I wanted out of the "club." Who doesn't want out on occasion? But for the most part, I was a happy member. Here's the bigger picture: for more than half my life, I was a wife and that's who I was. So, to not be one all of a sudden was bizarre.

Funny thing is that, in so many ways, Mike prepared me well to be single. He taught me to always look on the bright side. He taught me to laugh a lot and to laugh at myself, and not to sweat the small stuff. He encouraged me to go after my dreams, to not be afraid to fall on my face; that it's okay to make mistakes. When I worried, he would say, "Have you prayed?" or "Let's pray," or he would remind me that our children were healthy and safe so nothing else really mattered. He knew my strengths and helped me become stronger. He knew my weaknesses and was never critical. He knew my greatest Love was Jesus and guided me back to Him when I went my own way. Mike gently led and directed me to be independent (but dependent on God) and strong—to be the very best "me" I could be. He empowered me!

This "new club" is not so bad. I'm feeling more and more comfortable here. That's what I say as I move my wedding band to my right hand.

P.S. I've been encouraged, well-directed, loved and empowered by another wonderful man my whole life: my dad. My dad and mom are my biggest cheerleaders and have been a constant source of support, love and prayer. Thanks, Dad and Mom! And thank you to all the men out there who empower the women in their lives— daughters, sisters, friends and wives … we thank you!

Good men help make the women in their lives the best they can be (and vice versa).

Speaking of good men, just two weeks after I wrote "Good Men Empower Women," a great man, our dear friend Neil, passed away. In a post from back in April of 2012, I wrote about meeting him and his wife Donna for the first time after having become friends on Facebook.

This was my closing paragraph:

When Neil told us they were coming for a visit, he said we would have some laughs at his and Mike's expense. He was right. Here's an example of what he meant—Neil told us of the time he fell and broke three ribs (that, of course isn't the funny part). We laughed when he said he called Donna at work and told her not to worry, that the ambulance was on its way. We compared stories and had lots of laughs … a few somber moments, too, and we prayed. We had a wonderful time together and then they were on their way.

The day Neil reached out to me was a blessed day indeed! It was instant friendship, like acquiring a brother. He sent me a message and asked if I was the one with the ALS with Courage blog; the one with the husband with ALS. He explained that he had PLS (Primary Lateral Sclerosis) which is a disease closely related to ALS, and that he had many of the same symptoms Mike had. Sadly, Neil's illness transitioned to ALS shortly after we met.

When he and Donna came over for the first time, it was like welcoming sunshine. An abundance of joy and love accompanied them. Laughter filled the room. Our spirits improved.

Neil was funny, just so naturally witty. He brought comic relief in the middle of a battle with a killer disease. He and Mike were a lot alike humour-wise, so positive and strong in faith. As couples go, we were a match made in heaven. After that first visit, we all agreed we were family.

Neil emailed us a host of jokes, comics and funny stories, and once in a while he'd send a plea for prayer. He shared on a few occasions that he was afraid he sometimes took out his frustration on his beloved Donna. There was so much pain in those pleas. We assured him that Donna, so full of patience and grace, understood and that God's love covered over a multitude of frustrations.

We prayed for them and they prayed for us. The following is one of the last emails we received—specially addressed to Mike from June 2014:

"Hi Mike, I just wanted to say a big thank you for joining our team's ALS walk in Abbotsford last Saturday. Just you and Nadine being there was such an encouragement for me and Donna. We think very highly of you both and your faith is, well, extraordinary! Your smile is infectious, Mike, and know this: we never cease praying for your comfort, peace and rest!

That goes double for Nadine because, as you and I know, our wives deserve much better than what they're facing with us fighting this goofy disease! I'll sign off for now but not before I ask God to give you two a wonderful, restful sleep. Love you both, Neil."

Isn't God good, how He gives us friends we can relate with and people to grieve with, to laugh and cry with, to encourage and pray with, to be lifted by and to lift?

Shades of Yellow - June 3, 2016

It's definitely been a while since my last blog post. I wrote one, but it just didn't make the cut. Then I re-wrote it and, well, I'm contemplating if it makes the cut. Here's the thing, I'm at a place in my life where I'm wondering if I should just live it, not necessarily write about it and post it on the internet (for a while anyway).

Mike and I agreed if telling our story helped even one person, it was well worth it. I know it has helped many people and I am humbled and overjoyed about that. Along with helping others, my blog has helped me. It's been cheap therapy, so thanks for reading! Seriously though, it's been one lesson after another. The Lord has spoken to me as He has directed my writing. He has used it to strengthen my faith, to help me grow and heal and know Him more. I am so thankful for that. This experience has been such a blessing!

So anyway, here goes—my revised blog post. I anticipate a lesson or two for me by the time it's complete and I hope you enjoy. The title has changed a few times, but the smile that comes to my face ultimately makes the decision. "Shades of Yellow," is perfect. Here goes...

I've never had a cup of coffee in my life. I go out for "coffee" with friends sometimes, and weekly with my parents and sister, but I choose a different beverage. Not tea because I don't drink tea either, sometimes just water.

I remember from a young age, my parents being coffee drinkers. It was common to see my mom with a coffee cup in hand during the early hours of the day. She'd often forget where she placed her coffee as she went about her morning routine. It's actually a great memory. A few times I asked for a sip, and with a sour face I'd say, "How can you drink this?" She told me it was something you had to acquire a taste for. That's when I learned the meaning of "acquire a taste" and wondered why anyone would want to acquire a taste for coffee.

A few months ago, I went for coffee with a new friend. "Coffee" turned into dinner and a three-and-a-half-hour conversation. It didn't take long for me to realize he's the type of guy who could sweep a girl right off her feet. I went home and searched my closet for heavier shoes. Later, I wondered, *Was that a date?*

I was barely eighteen when Mike swept me off my feet. After our first date, he wanted me to be his girlfriend. I told him I was too young for a serious relationship. He didn't try to talk me into anything; instead he took out one of my closest friends. He knew I'd be at his place with his roommates and others that night socializing, so he came in holding my friend's hand. I was infuriated, and when I took him aside to confront him he replied something like, "You didn't want a serious boyfriend." His plan worked and by the end of the night, I was his girlfriend ... that was almost thirty years ago.

I grieved the loss of Mike over the course of his illness and I've grieved throughout the seventeen months since he passed away, and even though I still grieve, the Lord has recently given me new hopes and dreams, causing me to believe I could fall in love again.

It's remarkable how God redeems things, including hopes and dreams. He has proved this in my life many times.

At the author event I was a part of back in April at Whitby's bookstore in White Rock, B.C., the three of us authors there were asked what inspired our book titles. I shared that when I wrote my blog post "Hold On and Let Go" in February 2014, I thought it was the perfect title for our story and imagined it on the cover of a book someday (it became *Hold On, Let Go - Facing ALS with Courage and Hope* over a year now already). Anyway, in this post I mention how God redeems things. Here is part of that post:

People say what a difficult time we must be going through, but I don't feel like that at all. It's been difficult at times, but not necessarily a difficult time. It's been a time to grow and to learn. It's been a time to put things in proper perspective. It's a process for sure, but we are learning to hold on and let go. We let go of things in our lives that hinder and distract us like worry and fear, and hold on to things that enhance and beautify our lives like faith, hope, and love and all the other wonderful outpourings of the Lord.

Good things come from bad things all the time. That's how God works. He redeems things. God has done it with ALS in our lives a lot. I am constantly reminded of the Bible verse Romans 8:28, which says, "And we know that in all things God works for the good of those who love Him, who have been called according to his purpose."

Not long ago, I received a message from Leah's mom, Katrina. She stated, "I was talking to Leah this evening about her favourite colours and she told me that they are green, purple, and red. She also said that she loves yellow too, because it was Granddad's favourite colour. It's the colour of sunshine and it's a happy colour. She told me that when she used to pick candies from his candy bowl, she always chose the yellow ones." In another message, Katrina told me that Leah was still saving her yellow candies for Granddad.

I really appreciated this message, but the way Leah remembers the story isn't quite right. This is how the story goes. When Leah was little, she always chose the red, purple or orange-coloured candies. Mike took the yellow ones because the yellow ones were her least favourite. Leah eventually assumed that Granddad's favourite colour was yellow. Mike wasn't actually that fond of the colour yellow. I found that out one day after painting all the rooms in our house various shades of yellow. While standing there with a paint roller covered in something called Lemon Drops or Sunshine on My

Shoulder, Mike passed by and said that he never really cared much for yellow.

Anyway, Leah continued to save all her yellow candies for Granddad long after he stopped eating. She'd come in and hand Mike some yellow skittles or a yellow sucker that I intercepted and put in a dish and kept in a cupboard. Soon, she just took them straight to the cupboard. The collection of yellow candy grew over time, there was even a yellow feather in there. The dish was a little gift of sunshine and so is our darling Leah (who recently turned seven).

Mike and Leah (age 2) with suckers
- colours yellow and oranage.

"How wonderful the colour yellow is. It stands for the sun."
Vincent van Gogh

CHAPTER 11
The Most Beautiful Mayday Since 1948

"Consider it pure joy, my brothers and sisters, whenever you face trials of many kinds, because you know that the testing of your faith produces perseverance. Let perseverance finish its work so that you may be mature and complete, not lacking anything."

James 1:2-4 (NIV)

Most of the journal entries I've shared so far are from the first year of Mike's diagnosis. After that first year, I only journaled sporadically. The following is one of those entries:

Journal entry from Sept 27, 2014

The end is near. I just keep praying for more time. Mike had a rough day, which unfortunately now is very common. He had trouble breathing and clearing saliva. In the bathroom on his commode (after his morning enema), he struggled for a long time. But in the middle of it all, in what I would call peaceful turmoil, he asked, "How was your class?" referring to the fitness class I taught earlier that morning.

~

Honestly, it was never about him. He didn't dwell on his situation. He stayed calm; he thought beyond himself and his illness. He thought about me and others and I can only

145

imagine the praying that went on in his head. He was always an unselfish person; during his battle with ALS, he displayed the greatest selflessness, contentment and surrender I've ever encountered.

In the previous chapter, I ended the last blog post "Shades of Yellow" part way. I felt like the chapter was long enough, so I stopped in what I thought was a good spot and am picking up here from where I left off. If you happened to put the book down after the last chapter and need a refresher, here is what's happening: I went on a coffee date with a man and realized the potential of falling in love again. I don't say it's with Chris in my post, but I've already let you know. I share how I'm taking a break from blogging, I also rejoice in God's redemptive power and the wonderful colour of yellow...

Shades of Yellow - June 3, 2016 continued

When Karen brought up the topic of love in conversation a while ago, I told her I wasn't going to look for love, but if love found me, I would be open to it. When I think back on our conversation, my heart didn't necessarily agree with that statement the way my head did. Recently though, it's like the Lord opened the curtains of my heart and various shades of sunshine poured in. In that same conversation, Karen talked about Mike's love for me and how excellent, how deep, how selfless it was and how happy he'd be if love found me again when I am ready. I just smiled. I had no idea my heart was being made ready, and since then has come alive with the butterflies that now reside there again.

Shortly after the coffee date with my new friend, I contemplated the unexpected connection we had and was experiencing some mixed emotions, to say the least. I was looking for some advice ... for my beloved Mike's advice. I said to God, "What would Mike tell me?" Without hesitation, I heard, "You are worth far more than rubies. Remember what you are worth."

These words come from Proverbs 31:10-21:

"A woman of noble character who can find? She is worth far more than rubies...

She is clothed with strength and dignity; she can laugh at the days to come.

She speaks with wisdom, and faithful instruction is on her tongue...

Many women do noble things, but you surpass them all.

Charm is deceptive, and beauty is fleeting;

but a woman who fears the Lord is to be praised..."

It's funny because this Scripture crossed my mind while I wrote my last post "Good Men Empower Women." It's wonderful advice to pass on to all the women in my life.

Feeling valued beyond words and overwhelmed by God's extravagant love, I give thanks to Him for His healing power and the hope and joy He's poured into my life, and for all of His provisions. He knows my needs far better than I do and He is always faithful to provide ... and He continues to redeem things.

Only the Lord knows what my future holds concerning my writing (and everything else in my life, of course). I love writing and don't plan to give it up but wonder if this is a good place to stop (or just take a break from this ALS With Courage story).

To all of you who have been touched by ALS, you are like brothers and sisters to me. And to everyone, including friends and family and those I've never met, God bless you and thanks for your encouragement and support!

"Each of us may be sure that if God sends us on stony paths, He will provide us with strong shoes and He will not send us out on any journey for which He does not equip us well."

Alexander Maclaren

In closing, I will wish a happy birthday to my mom (June 1st). Here is another wonderful memory of my mom and coffee: Mom and I have done a lot of painting together. Not pictures, but walls—you know, rooms. We have painted each other's places (way more mine than hers). We have painted a bunch of rooms in my sister's house and some for friends. It's always been so much fun. And when I think of those times, this is what I see—my mom with a paint brush in one hand and a coffee cup in the other and a huge smile on her face and tons of laughter. She's a woman who lives to help her kids, grandkids and others. She's a woman of noble character. She is clothed with strength and dignity. She speaks with wisdom and faithful instruction is on her tongue. She is a woman who fears the Lord, a woman to be praised. Thanks, Mom and Dad, for your steadfast love and all your prayers and encouragement!

This picture speaks of the love and support:

Dad, Elanna, Mom and me at the ALS Society of B.C. recognition night, where I received the Exceptional Advocacy award. I didn't think I deserved it but accepted it with honour on behalf of my whole family. It's definitely a team effort.

All of us at the ALS Walk, 2013

I was falling in love with the man I went out for coffee with in my "Shades of Yellow" story, and knew I needed to take a break from blogging. I wanted to keep my relationship with Chris quiet. It wasn't a secret; I just didn't think it was in good taste to advertise it. I knew some people in my life weren't ready to watch me move on. I later explain that I will never move on from Mike, but I will try to keep moving forward in my life.

Although the relationship grew quickly, I was definitely very guarded at first. I kept in mind the words I got from the Lord when I asked for advice from Mike. "Remember your worth—you are worth far more than rubies" stuck with me. I kept thinking I needed to protect myself. I needed to be very careful not to settle for anything less than God's best. I wanted to make the right decision, of course. A few months later, as quickly as that message came, so did another. That next message was this: "It wasn't a warning; it was a reminder." Wow, was I humbled! God was protecting and guarding me. He knows my worth. I'm His daughter and He's my perfect Father, and as I had prayed and prayed I was reminded He'd never lead me astray.

So much happened during that year off from my blog. I fell in love and got engaged. My mom was diagnosed with cancer and passed away. Two friends with ALS also passed away, one the day my mom passed and one a month later.

You and Me and a Cherry Blossom Tree
- June 14, 2017

It's late, really late. I hesitate to look at the time. I'm tired but I can't sleep. Different sounds and shadows of trees on my new bedroom wall are just a couple of things among many that keep me from sleeping. Also, and mostly, thoughts of my mom have come on strong.

I keep putting this off—writing, that is. I procrastinate, but tonight feels right to get started. I check Facebook...Instagram...email...Facebook again. Then, all of a sudden, here I am. Almost instantly I feel like that caged bird set free. My soaring skills are a little rusty, but the joy of writing feels just the same. It feels like home to me.

If you are, or were, a regular reader of my blog, you will have noticed it's been a while since I posted my last piece—just over a year, actually. It doesn't mean I haven't written anything. My list of writing projects of the past twelve months include a couple of letters to the local newspaper editor, my mom's obituary and eulogy, a few emails I carefully composed, and most recently, wedding vows.

In my last blog post "Shades of Yellow" from June 2016, I mention that perhaps instead of writing about my life and sharing it on the internet, I would just live it. I knew in my heart that after almost five years of blogging, I needed to take a step back. Today, I take a step forward. Today, I pick up the proverbial pen again and let the words out.

Speaking of stepping forward, I got married

last month. I tried to keep the fact that I was seeing someone, and then engaged, quiet. I wasn't shouting the news from any mountaintops like an excited bride-to-be would. I was quietly telling close friends when I saw them. The reason I kept things under wraps is because not everyone in my life was ready for it. Me moving forward was okay, but giant leaps like this one were a little hard to take. I tried to keep the cat in the bag on my Facebook page, but the cat was let out of the bag shortly before the big day, and then pictures of us, the bride and groom, were shared and the "cat" had long run away. It actually brought me some relief. I had to just let it be; after all, this is my new reality.

I agree it happened really fast. I wasn't looking for love, but love found me. I'll share how that happened shortly, but what I wondered is, how could I love another so quickly when my heart still aches for Mike? How could I "move on" with another man when I was still grieving the loss of the love of my life?

Grief is a funny thing. Not funny "haha," but funny in how it's hard to define—mysterious, kind of; not concrete. It can be extremely complicated and just so simple sometimes. It's different for every person. It comes in all shapes and sizes and is not constrained to any timelines. After a while it lightens up, but unexpectedly becomes heavy again. You can stuff it down, hide it away, lock it up and throw away the key, but like Houdini, it eventually has to breathe, and it has a magic way with locks and things. It can be sharp like broken glass and prickly like a cactus and sometimes soft like the pillow upon which you lay your head and cry yourself to sleep. It can be the ugliest monster you've ever seen, but ultimately pretty. It's exceptionally beautiful, actually … that is, if and when you receive the healing it's meant to bring.

I sure have learned a lot about it over the last few years. It's been a journey of grieving since I first heard the words amyotrophic lateral sclerosis. Some might think that I've finished grieving Mike's death and ALS because I got married again, but that's not true. In fact, since meeting Chris I've grieved deeply. We both have. I think we both have received a lot of healing in grieving together. I touch on it in my wedding vows. Part of my vows go like this:

Chris, you know I have struggled with the timing of us. But I needed to trust God and, of course, I couldn't fight the love. Something special happened the moment I first heard your voice, and in an instant you were my friend. By the end of the conversation, I was smitten. The love grew in leaps and bounds as I got to know you. I didn't think I needed anyone, but God knows what we need better than we do. He provided someone to help bear the burden of my grief, except it wasn't a burden for you, it was a blessing because you were grieving, too. It's been something extremely beautiful. His joy feels complete in me but continues to increase. He is just so faithful! He is a God of extravagant love and that love and all His glory is on display today as we come together as one. I look so forward to continuing this journey with you, with the Lord as our guide. And I will strive and rely on Him to help me be the wife He desires me to be for you.

The healing process is a marvellous one, but it doesn't mean I'm over Mike. On the contrary, I miss him more than ever and he's never felt more a part of me than he does right now.

The road of grieving, for me, has taken many twists and turns recently. My mom's passing in November still leaves me and my family speechless and in disbelief. Since she passed away, my poor dad has also lost a sister and a brother. We stick close and are there for each other, but some days I struggle just to keep my own head above water.

Other friends have passed as well—a few with ALS, including our dear pal Randy who I'll tell you about at a later date, and Darryl who I've mentioned in my writing before. When it comes to ALS, I've said it a few times: I'm in it for life … in whatever capacity and for however long the Lord wants me to be.

I'm thrilled to have my amazing partner Chris to continue on this journey with. I recently told him while I was hugging him that sometimes when I'm hugging him, I'm actually holding on for dear life.

Here is part of our story. This is what we shared in our wedding brochure:

To tell our story is to tell of Him…

Chris says:
When my wife Heather, who was very ill with cancer, took her daily afternoon nap, I'd go out to clear my head. One day while browsing aimlessly in the House

of James bookstore in Abbotsford where we lived, I saw Nadine's book. On a wall of about thirty books, hers was the only one I could see. I was drawn to the picture of love on the cover and the title Hold On, Let Go. It looked like a story that could help me. I put it down and thought I'd get it another time. When I went back the next day, it was sold out. I ordered a copy and when it arrived two weeks later, Heather's health had declined further, and I was afraid of what that book was going to tell me (that was in July 2015). The book sat on my table for three months. Heather passed away in August, we had her memorial service in September, and in October I traveled to Ontario to visit relatives—I took the book to read. There were a lot of similarities in our stories and a lot of healing in Nadine's writing for me. Five months later, I reached out to Nadine in a letter to thank her for sharing her and Michael's story...

Nadine says:

It was about 9:00 p.m. and I was curled up on my couch, contemplating the speech I was giving at a conference the next day. I was a little overcome with some negative thoughts, like who would want to hear me speak anyway? This is a big mistake, and so on. I was praying and battling those kinds of lies. Right when I needed it most, I received a Facebook message from a man I didn't know. It was a beautiful letter. He explained who he was and told me about his wife and their journey with terminal cancer, and how she passed away a few months after Mike. He told the story of how he found my book and how it ministered to him and how he wanted to meet me and thank me in person. Unfortunately, he was unable to attend the conference because he had to work, but he wished me well and said he'd be praying for me. His letter really encouraged me, and the negative thoughts disappeared. The timing of Chris' letter was perfect…

Chris says:

I wanted to hear Nadine's speech, so I asked her to speak at my church. We talked about it on the phone and agreed on a day a couple of months away. There was an instant connection when we spoke. I planned to go to another author event she was going to be at in White Rock, but couldn't wait the few weeks to meet. So I took a chance and asked her out for coffee. She accepted, and our "coffee" turned into a three-and-a-half-hour dinner date. At one point, Nadine started professing her deep love for Jesus. I was speechless and a little in awe because shortly after Heather passed away, I started praying that when the time was right, and if there was ever going to be another woman in my life, the Lord would bring one with a huge heart for Jesus. I knew then that Nadine was the answer to my prayer, and I started praying that her heart would be opened to me…

Nadine says:

I had some walls up, for sure, and I thought it was too soon, but the Lord's timing is always right, and I quickly knew Chris was a gift from Him. March 4th (2016) was the day I received Chris' letter. "March forth" is a message we have taken to heart. Even though we will never "move on" from Heather and Mike—they will always have a place in our hearts and in our lives—we keep "moving forward" in God's plans as He directs and guides. We aren't finished grieving and we may never be, but to grieve together is such a wonderful blessing. With indescribable joy, love and peace, we look forward to serving the Lord together and experiencing all He has in store for us as husband and wife.

We didn't plan it, but there we were under a beautiful cherry blossom tree in the park where we had our wedding photos taken. As our photographer snapped pictures, a mysterious breeze swept in and gently blew the pinkish hued petals off the tree—they just floated in the air all around us. I said to Chris, "You know Mike and I had a thing for cherry blossom trees, right?" With a big "Wow, this-is-kind-of-crazy" smile, he replied, "Yes, I do know that." Later, we agreed it was like Mike showed up, or at least he was sending a message. I feel like the blossoms were his blessing.

I just read this about the cherry blossom tree in a Huffpost article titled "The Significance of the Cherry Blossom - From Beloved Tree to Cultural Icon." The author, Homaro Cantu, states: "In Japan, the cherry blossom represents the fragility and the beauty of life." He explains that the tree is considered a visual reminder that life is precious and exceedingly beautiful, but it is also uncertain and "tragically short."

Under that tree, I felt like Mike was saying to me, "You are right where you are meant to be." I felt absolutely surrounded by his love, Chris' love, and, ultimately, the impeccable love of God.

It's funny because the original plan for the cover of my book *Hold On, Let Go* was to be a picture of cherry blossoms—it was in the works. But through a series of events, a picture of me and Mike ended up on the cover instead, which is what ultimately drew Chris to my book.

"Oh, how great are God's riches and wisdom and knowledge! How impossible it is for us to understand His decisions and His ways! For everything comes from Him and exists by His power and is intended for His glory. All glory to Him forever! Amen."
Romans 11:33,36 (NLT)

After working on this piece for over a week, I post it today—June 14th, Chris' birthday. Happy birthday, Chris! I wish you a year filled with abundant joy, surpassing peace, and lots and lots of love and laughter! Thank you for embracing me and my love story. Thanks for being a listening ear, a shoulder for my tears, and a pillar for me to lean on. Thanks for your patience, understanding, kindness and incredible love! You are a gift from above!

Side note: I call our wedding day (May 6th) the most beautiful Mayday since 1948 when my mom was May Queen of Port Coquitlam, B.C. After telling my friend Shayna, who offered to help plan and decorate for our wedding, that we had promised my mom she'd be there (not knowing how little time she had left), Shayna added the most beautiful touches of my mom, including ribbons on sticks that were waved by our guests, and ribbons in the trees which were a magical touch indeed.

In my last post "Shades of Yellow," Chris is the man I met for coffee. Wow, what can happen in a year...

I dedicate this post to my mom, who loved without walls, fences, limits or conditions. Her love was like our Father's love and I am forever grateful and inspired to love like she did.

"God is love, and whoever abides in love abides in God, and God in him."

1 John 4:16 (ESV)

Our wedding was truly beautiful, but if I could rewind time there are things I would do differently. I don't think I was in the right frame of mind to plan a wedding. Thankfully, God provided Shayna.

I wasn't excited about planning a wedding, considering not everyone was ready for it and my mom had recently passed away. I wasn't even telling people about our engagement. While out walking somewhat aimlessly one day (in early January), I dropped in to see a few of my favourite ladies at the Tea and Gift shop I love called, Once Upon a Tea Leaf on 224th Street. Shayna works there on Saturdays, Cindy is the owner and Taryn is Cindy's daughter. It's a wonderful place to go for a cup of tea, a beautiful gift or if you just need to be uplifted.

We got talking about how our Christmases went and I decided to show them the engagement ring that I received. Well, that was it. After the cheering and congratulating, the planning began. Taryn had me hooked up with a makeup/hair person and a photographer before I left. Shayna told me about all the wonderful things she had from another wedding she recently planned. I knew I was in good hands.

Shayna, who is already extremely busy, took her offer to help with our wedding seriously and insisted it was her gift to me. She recruited her husband Roger, and together they worked really hard and assured us it was a blessing for them and a way to serve God. During the planning stage, they invited us over to their place to show us some of the things they had in store for our big day. When we stepped into their home, we were blown away. They had all their excellent ideas out on display so we could decide on this, that and the other lovely thing. It was tempting to scrap the church wedding with eighty-person guest list and say our "I do's" right there and then. If we had had someone to officiate, maybe we would have. But I had already eloped once, so this time, in honour of my mom, I was having a traditional wedding.

Shayna and Roger set everything up the night before the wedding and the morning of ... with a little bit of help from us. The flower arrangements and bouquets were amazing, along with the candy buffet, shelves they made for the cupcakes, vintage furniture and other vintage touches, pictures and mementos of my mom's, and, of course, ribbons tied to branches in the magnolia tree out front and other hints of Mayday.

The evening of the day my mom had her chemotherapy, when everyone had left the hospital except for me and Chris, she wanted to talk. She took her subtle innuendo about a wedding to the next level. She came right out and asked when we were getting engaged. Even though Chris had already proposed, we weren't telling anybody. We assured her that we were definitely going to get married and she'd be the first to know. She also had us promise she'd be there, even if in a wheelchair. Sadly, that promise we couldn't keep.

Chris had asked me to marry him in September at a Rob Thomas concert (Chris had arranged for Rob to video the proposal during the meet and greet), but like I said, we didn't tell anyone. I didn't even tell my sister or my mom, knowing a secret like that would be difficult to keep. Chris and I had discussed marriage and we both felt that was God's plan for us, and as creative and special as his proposal was, it was too soon —or so I thought. We decided we would announce the engagement at a later date, giving our children more time to get used to our fast-moving relationship.

When the doctors informed us that the chemo was causing Mom's organs to shut down and that she was going to pass away, we showed her the video of Chris' proposal that day. She was the first to know and she was elated. Sure enough, the next nurse to come in and doctor and everyone within earshot heard all about it.

Even though Mom didn't make it to our wedding, it was

planned with her foremost in mind. Shayna made sure Mom was honoured there, along with Chris' parents who are both gone. Everything Shayna took on was exceptionally well done. People still rave about the beautiful ambience she created, as well as the incredible food catered by my friend Michelle; the cupcakes in a variety of delicious flavours by Katrina and my friend Denise, and the John Wayne groom's cake by Madison.

Indeed, the most beautiful Mayday since 1948.

Wedding photo by Warin Marie Photography

CHAPTER 12
Gluten-Free Pancakes and a Lost Girl Like Me

"Deep calls to deep in the roar of Your waterfalls;
all Your waves and breakers have swept over me."
Psalm 42:7 (NIV)

From my mom's eulogy:

Jesus and family was everything to Mom. She was known to show family pictures to complete strangers. She was also known for her amazing laugh, beautiful blue eyes, abounding love and long goodbyes. Her claim to fame: May Queen of Port Coquitlam, B.C., 1948.

A few days before our mom passed away, we had music playing in her hospital room. A song called "The Only Name" by Big Daddy Weave came on. It sings of His name that saves us, His mercy and grace that forgave us and that His love is all we need. I sang along in Mom's ear so she would be clear on all the words. She whispered back "I've been thinking that all day."

Mom had B-cell lymphoma; we had no idea how aggressive it was. We watched her health decline right in front of us. Before she went into the hospital, Dad took great care of her at home. Mom raved about his wonderful caregiving and how attentive he was to her every need.

Mom spent two weeks in hospital. While there, she had one chemo treatment that caused her to go into renal failure and she passed away just over a week later. A day and a half before she left us, she said her goodbyes. It was so sad, of course, but it was also a joyful time. There was a lot of hugging and kissing, laughing and crying, and some last words. She called us all her "treasure." She was excited to go home to be with Jesus and see beloved family and friends there.

Our mom had a good life. Her perspective made it good, her attitude made it great and her faith made it exceptional. Her priorities were love and laughter, prayer and serving others.

Appropriately born in springtime; a ray of sunshine to say the least. The Lord blessed this planet and her parents Loyola and Ted Wald with her presence in 1937. She became a stellar big sister to three siblings.

She had such fond memories of growing up next door to cousins, of tap dance and violin lessons, of helping her mom with chores and babysitting and of becoming owner/operator of an ice cream shop her dad built for her on their front yard: Sheila's Ice Cream and Confectionary.

She laughed when she reminisced about childhood memories and all her dad's pranks. One of my personal favourites is the story of when Grandpa rigged the toilet seat so that when someone sat down, the doorbell rang. The person sitting on the toilet would get up and answer the door and find no one there. They returned to the washroom to repeat the process.

He was a real prankster and extremely kindhearted. As an electrician, he did a lot of work pro bono for customers who struggled financially. Mom started working at a bank at a young age to help out. Her face lit up when she talked about buying her parents their first refrigerator along with other appliances and household necessities. On payday, she was thrilled to purchase her brothers and sister new clothes and other things.

Mom met Dad at a dance. Soon after they got married, they started a family. When Elanna came along, Sheila Mary Klassen began her journey of becoming the world's greatest mom. She and Dad experienced a tremendous loss when Mom gave birth a second time to a stillborn. Mom talked about how Elanna, just a tyke, made her peanut butter and jam sandwiches to help during that very painful time. After that great loss and a miscarriage, I came along, and I could not have been more loved. I have felt adored all my life.

We moved to Maple Ridge in 1977, and mom's commute to her job at the Scotiabank in Port Coquitlam became a little longer; she didn't mind. Mom loved her job as a bank teller. With many opportunities to climb the proverbial ladder, she remained a teller because of the social interaction it offered. She loved people and she loved serving others. As I worked my way through the lineup at the bank, I'd often hear people say, "Feel free to go ahead of me. I'm waiting for Sheila." And I'd be like, "Same here." Mom was held up—yes, robbed—a record five times. One robber wrote her a note to apologize and thank her for being so kind. She retired from the bank in 2001 ... unscathed.

Mom's life exploded with joy when she became a grandma, and she loved nothing more than to brag about her grandchildren and great-granddaughter. She attended as many games, concerts, races, tournaments, plays, recitals, speeches and ceremonies as possible. She liked to cut their hair when they were little and take them shoe shopping. She dropped everything to pick them up from school or take them to a practice or to work or anywhere.

Mom was raised in a God-fearing home and went to church faithfully all her life. But it wasn't until she was in her mid-forties that she committed her whole life to Jesus Christ … she made her knowledge and belief in God a relationship of the heart. Her faith and love for the Lord continued to grow over the years.

Mom and Dad became missionaries in their late forties, showing the Jesus Film on the Amazon River. They founded their society, Amazon Evangelism, and spent many years traveling to Brazil to share the Gospel message. Later, they started drilling wells and providing for the needs of orphans in Malawi, Africa through Project Wellness (a division of Amazon Evangelism). Dad continues the good work at the seasoned age of almost eighty.

Mom didn't have a selfish bone in her body. She excelled in patience. She was an outstanding cheerleader. She was a prayer warrior. She prayed every day for every family member and many friends and people she didn't know. Mom and Dad made it a priority to pray together daily as well. She and Dad continued their appliance and gift giving throughout their lives together while on a modest budget. Mom carried gloves in her car for anyone she saw riding a bicycle in the cold weather. She always said she hated to see frozen hands on handlebars.

Our mom was such a bright light, a blessing to know, an exquisite soul … always and forever our May Queen!

Mom as May Queen 1948

A Lost Girl Like Me (Deep Calls to Deep)
- Aug 16, 2017

Chris and I both cried our way through breakfast the other day. While I choked down my delicious gluten-free pancakes, I watched Chris devour his sausage and cheese omelet, and at the same time continuously wipe tears away. It's like they just wouldn't stop. We didn't stop either. We kept eating like nothing was wrong … this sort of thing isn't that uncommon. Before the server delivered our meal, Chris started tearing up. When I questioned him, he said he saw a couple walk in and the woman clearly had cancer.

Chris and I traveled down the Oregon Coast this past week—kind of like part two of our honeymoon. For me, it was a dream come true; Chris had been before. The breakfast I'm telling you about took place in a town where Chris and Heather spent a couple of days, three years ago. Chris showed me the hotel where they stayed and a few other memorable places. The Pig N Pancake restaurant where we were eating was where they ate. Hence, the opened floodgates when the women who seemingly had cancer walked through the door. Chris explained, "This is my Victoria."

A week after our wedding, Chris and I went to Victoria, B.C., for his aunt's surprise birthday party. It was a quick trip because Chris had sold his house and had to be out that same weekend. We stayed one night and took in a few sights, and everything we saw reminded me of Mike. He and I spent a lot of time there together over the years—sometimes just the two of us, sometimes with the kids, and always when his mum vacationed there from Toronto visiting her sister and brothers. I loved it but had no idea it was going to hit me so hard. Chris watched me wipe away many tears those couple of days as I was overwhelmed with the plethora of memories.

The thing is, away or at home, I'm constantly reminded of Mike, and if it's not tears on my face it's a big smile. Every once in a while I ask Chris if he's getting tired of hearing about Mike. The last time I asked, he responded "Never." Chris has really gotten to know Mike and likes getting to know him better. I feel the same about Heather. She was an incredible woman, someone I would have been honoured to call my friend. As weird as it sounds, I feel a strong connection.

Anyway, back to the Pig N Pancake. Here's the

thing. When Chris started tearing up, so did I. Just when the tears where welling in my eyes, the server brought our food. I had never ordered pancakes before; my mom ordered them all the time. She loved pancakes, and when my pancakes were placed in front of my face so were many beloved thoughts of her. In that moment, I missed her more than ever.

I felt completely numb the morning my mom died. I had stayed with her overnight like a couple of other times, but this one was different. She had been moved from a hospital room of four to a room for one at the end of the hall. It felt like the end-of-the-line kind of room. Chris stayed, too. We tried to get comfortable on the skinny cot the nurse brought, but this night wasn't about getting a good sleep, or any sleep; this night was about watching and waiting and praying … this night was about a final so-long.

If I hadn't already decided to marry Chris before this, my decision would have been made and the deal would have been sealed right then. Since meeting him, he had already absorbed hundreds of my tears on various sleeves as I continued to grieve Mike's death, and now he held me up as I realized my mom's last breath had come and gone.

My mom had a short battle with cancer. How long for sure, we don't really know. From diagnosis it was less than two months, and ultimately the chemotherapy killed her. She was in the hospital for two weeks. Elanna, and I agree that sharing a lot of the constant care she needed was a marvellous gift. It was a drop in the bucket of payback to the lifetime of care she gave us. We all did everything in our power to keep her comfortable as she endured the side effects of the chemo and, sadly, the shutting down of her kidneys and other major organs.

Numb is the word I use to describe how I felt the morning she died. Today, I think I feel the same way. It happened so fast. She was at a fitness class a few weeks before she went into the hospital. Watching my dad grieve the passing of the love-of-his-life for over fifty-five years has been painful enough. My grieving had to be delayed. I'm still shaking my head and questioning, *Is she really gone?*

When I see a freshly-made bed, for a split second I think, *My mom's been here.* Same thing when I see "Mom and Dad" on my cell phone call display. From one extreme of elation to the immediate opposite of deepest disappointment, I sadly remember she's gone. Elanna shared recently that she went into her laundry room and saw freshly-ironed clothing hanging there, and her first thought was, *Mom was here!* Then instantly that sinking feeling crept in of, *No, she's gone.*

I've been feeling a little lost lately, sometimes more than others. I guess the feeling kind of comes and goes. It's mostly my heart and head that feel lost, and my feet sometimes as I often question, *What am I doing here again?* After Mike passed away, I felt that way a lot.

For a long time, I blamed my scattered thoughts, memory loss and inability to focus on the grieving process. Then about a year ago, I was like, wait a minute:

perimenopause! Lately, the above feelings have been mixed with the feelings you get when you're a little girl separated from your mom at the mall for too long—discontentment, anxiety, fear and so on. I describe it in one word: lost. And even though I'm all grown up now and I'm less afraid, I've decided the longer the separation from my mom, the more I feel this way.

As I ponder this lost place, God has met me in it with His comfort, guidance and grace, and I've heard Him speak "Deep calls to deep." The first time I heard it, I thought of Canadian Christian artist Steve Bell's beautiful acoustic arrangement of, "Deep Calls to Deep" (adapted by Steve Bell, original author unknown). My friend Suzy, most definitely his biggest fan, got me hooked on him. She invited me, Elanna and our mom to one of his concerts years ago, and I was struck by the lyrics: "Deep calls to deep and my soul finds no resting place but Him. He is my God, the yearning of my soul His touch can still. And each rare moment, I felt His presence, I shall remember and forever cherish…"

Since then, we've been to a few with her and other friends (she always saves us front row seats). Anyway, I knew "Deep calls to deep" was part of a verse I was pretty sure found in the book of Psalms. Indeed, chapter 42, verse 7 says: "Deep calls to deep in the roar of your waterfalls; all your waves and breakers have swept over me." (NIV)

My first thought was that the deep things of God call out to the deep things of me (and vice versa sometimes), and the water from above flows into the waters below. As this blended H2O washes over me, there's this deeper communing with my Lord, producing indescribable joy and peace ... something along those lines. I'm not a Bible scholar, but I've been there before and feel I'm just speaking from experience. I did a little research about how my take on the Psalmist's writing compares to others. There were some different ideas, but most included this idea of "communing"— deep communing with God.

Sometimes it just seems easier to stay in the shallow places. I think we all resist the "deep" for various reasons. The deep can be scary; the fear of the unknown. It's beyond our comfort zone. We have to be more vulnerable there. We get stretched there. We have to listen and wait, and we wonder what He's going to say there. But when we let go and follow the call, agape love invades the soul and we are forever changed.

I've decided that this lost feeling is okay and is probably not going to change. I'm just passing through this place, and even though I love my life and want to fulfill all of God's plans for me here, I have a longing for my heavenly home. It's like a little piece of me is there already with Mom and Mike and others so dearly missed.

Recently while Dad, Elanna, Chris and I were gathered around a table with a friend in one of our favourite coffee shops, the friend asked us what was so great about heaven. What are we going to do in heaven? What's the big deal about heaven? I know the Bible has a lot of amazing descriptions of heaven and one of us could have really tried to sell it. Instead, what blurted out of my mouth was something like this: "Our Saviour and Lord is there – our best friend, Jesus. We look forward to seeing Him face to face and being in His presence."

If you are feeling like a lost little girl like me, don't worry. Follow the call as deep calls to deep!

God's peace!

"Friends, this world is not your home, so don't make yourselves cozy in it. Don't indulge your ego at the expense of your soul. Live an exemplary life..."
1 Peter 2:11 (Message)

I went to my mom's chemotherapy appointment with her. Elanna and Chris were with her at her last appointment, and we took turns with appointments as best we could. I took the day off work to accompany her to this one. I'm so glad I did.

We went by ambulance from the hospital in Maple Ridge to the Royal Columbian Hospital in New Westminster. She talked the ear off the ambulance attendant for the full forty minutes or so it took to get there; I sat in the front with the driver. Mom told the kind and very good listener all about my book, *Hold On, Let Go,* like she had with other people (including complete strangers) many times before, and then proceeded with my continued love story. Mom was a sucker for a good love story and an enthusiastic proclaimer of an awesome God story—and this, of course, was both.

We spent hours at the chemotherapy clinic, and I enjoyed every minute. Mom met so many wonderful people there and they all listened with interest to her go on again about my book and Chris and how we met and all about her other daughter and son-in-law, her husband, grandkids and so on. The nurses were fantastic and treated her so wonderfully. I brought some books I thought we could read, but we had no time for reading. There were too many people to converse with, including a woman we knew from years ago sitting next to Mom. And we had each other.

We talked about many things in between our lovely visits with all these new and old friends. She told me how she prayed every morning for every family member. She went through the lineup, from closest—her children and grandchildren, siblings and their children and grandchildren (on hers and Dad's side), and cousins and second cousins and all of their children and so on. She had such a strong faith and was sure all her prayers were heard and being answered. She was also open and vulnerable about what she wasn't sure of. I loved hearing every word. I'd give my right arm to do that day over again. Except knowing what I know now, I'd say, "Stop everything! Don't get the chemo!"

I knew from a young age my mom was exceptional. I remember my Auntie Vicki saying to me "Your mom is extra special" as we both watched her interacting at a family gathering. And I thought, *That's so true.* Joyful was an understatement. My childhood memories recall her singing and dancing a lot with her coffee cup in hand, or at the stove or just walking through the family room.

My mom doted on me more than anybody. I think after

losing two babies before me, it's what came naturally. I didn't always appreciate it, though; I actually didn't like it much at all. Of course, now I'd love to hear her say "poor baby" about a cold or cough or anything that slightly inconveniences me.

I didn't tell my mom everything like some daughters do with their mothers. I never wanted to worry or upset her. She was there for me to lean on and I didn't take full advantage of it. Don't get me wrong, she was a constant source of help and support. What I mean is, I didn't really confide in her about my struggles and troubles and cries of the heart. I wonder why sometimes. Did my pride get in the way, as though to say, *I can do it on my own?* Or did I underestimate her incredible strength and the depths of her faith? She could have handled anything. Needless to say, I punished both of us by keeping some distance when I was going through trials and experiencing pain.

I sometimes wonder about my mom's grief; the devastation of losing a baby. Two really, but this one full-term. A lifeless little body with a birthday that proceeded its date of death. This little one whose Mommy and Daddy had a lifetime of dreams and ideas laid out for, and a big sister who could hardly wait to hold and count ten perfect little toes. As I write this paragraph, I'm encountering a grief I've never experienced before. I'm sorrowful for maybe the first time about the loss of this unnamed older sibling, but more so for my mom's pain that I never really inquired about. I don't remember ever saying I was sorry. I was just a kid and what did I know? But now I know. The grief would have run deeper than I could ever imagine. She would have cried a million tears while we were oblivious. What brings joy in this sorrow that I now know, is the thought of Mom's arrival in heaven and meeting this beloved child for the first time.

I guess my mom was afraid of losing me before and after I was born. She, I'm sure, prayed every day that I would live—not just survive, but live—a really great life. I will forever cherish her incredible love and her faith-filled prayers for me (and others) which are still being answered to this day.

"My deep need calls out to the deep kindness of Your love.
Your waterfall of weeping sent waves of sorrow over my soul, carrying me away… Yet all day long God's promises of love pour over me. Through the night I sing His songs,
for my prayer to God has become my life."

I love the above Passion translation of the "deep calls to deep" verse in Psalm 42. The disparity of the two—the need of me and you, and the kindness of God's love—is so poetically put into perspective. It acknowledges that the need of the human being runs deep, but next to the endless depths of God's merciful love and intimacy it quickly recedes. Oh, how this rings profoundly with me. And the shallow things become shallower.

Mom in front of her store.

CHAPTER 13
Best Friends & PALs and Laying Your Burdens Down

"The Lord is my shepherd; I have all that I need.
He lets me rest in green meadows; He leads me beside peaceful
streams… He guides me along right paths bringing honour to
His name."

Psalm 23:1-2 (NLT)

I experience an extra measure of peace when I'm amongst trees. I think there is value in stopping for a moment to survey different patterns of bark, pinecones, and leaves. In my experience, giving a large trunk a big hug is therapy. There is a whole world in a tree and a reminder that the universe doesn't revolve around me. It's the same when I stand in the sand on the beach and let the ocean waters wash over my bare feet. I look out as far as the eye can see and my burdens get lighter in the expanse of His awesome creation.

One of Nathan's recent sermons titled, "Where to Find God," provided three suggestions; one of which was in nature. I certainly experience His strong presence there. Nature is fascinating, astonishing, sometimes jaw-dropping. It often renders me speechless outwardly and promotes cheering in my heart. It's art. There's mystery, sometimes suspense, birth, life, death—it gives us a glimpse of God's greatness and extreme detailed creativity and love.

Forests give Him standing ovations, crashing waves applaud Him, birds sing praises to His name; shouldn't we do the same?

Dances With Leaves - Nov 5, 2017

The way the sun has shone on the autumn leaves in the trees these past few weeks has got me dwelling on the extreme beauty this season brings. The sun is lower in the sky and instead of shining from above it comes in from the side like a spotlight and illuminates the brilliance of the simple, yet remarkably crafted, fragile leaf.

Fall captivates me; it romances me. It causes emotions to run wild in me. I liken it to the crescendo that bridges the third and fourth movements of Beethoven's fifth symphony. I'm not much of a classical music listener but this is the best way I can think to describe what this magical buildup to the passing of the life of the leaf is like. Whether it lets go of the tree or the branch sets it free, its graceful dancing descent in the breeze causes a dancing on the inside of me.

Eventually, the vibrant canopy that dazzled overhead becomes a lush, colourful carpet under feet. I love the variety of oranges and yellows and greens, but it's the deep reds that really mesmerize me and at the age of forty-nine, I'm like a kindergarten student again, collecting and examining leaves for the first time.

My aunt in hospice waits patiently for the Lord to

take her home. While Elanna and I were there visiting recently, she said she couldn't understand what the Lord was waiting for. Elanna told her that He has the exact perfect time in mind and explained He's most likely preparing her family to say goodbye; and He's still using her here to be a glorious witness for Him. Our aunt's reply: "Wow, really? Sounds good!"

It's been a huge blessing to spend more time with our aunt since her cancer diagnosis. Elanna and I have enjoyed our "girl time" with her in hospice and are reminded over and over again of our mom, who one year ago went to hospital to fight her own cancer battle. As heartbroken as I still am, I can't help but compare that experience, and now my aunt's, to the exquisite journey of the simple yet remarkably crafted, fragile leaf.

"To everything there is a season and a time to every purpose under heaven"
Ecclesiastes 3:1

I had to put a piece I've been working on for weeks on hold lately. I switched to this one about the leaf, not that this one was necessarily easy. I've been writing about my dear friend Randy. Every time I try and add a few sentences, I end up crying like a baby. I didn't realize how much grief I have stuffed. He passed away with ALS one month after my mom died. Anyway, writing about Randy, anticipating my mom's one-year anniversary, and spending time with my aunt in hospice lately is causing me to be slightly (and sometimes extremely) weepy and a little distracted, I guess. It doesn't help that I've recently binge-watched the show This Is Us. I was, and maybe still am, concussed and have a tendency to carry the weight of other people's burdens on my shoulders. I don't feel like the "Nadine who can do anything and everything." So friends and family, please be patient with me. In fact, let's be patient with everybody because you never know what the next person is going through.

In closing, the joy of the Lord is my strength! I am so grateful for the constant presence of the Lord in my life, and like Psalm 16:11 says, "In His presence there is fullness of joy." I'm always in awe of His beauty that surrounds me, and I wonder how anyone can ask "Where is He?" I find His strong presence there in nature. Whether I'm outside enveloped by His genius artistry or just looking through my window at the leaves blowing in the breeze, I'm forever saying "God, You're amazing!"

"Even when I walk through the darkest valley, I will not be afraid, for You are close beside me. Your rod and Your staff protect and comfort me."
Psalm 32:4 (NLT)

Journal entry from October 10, 2011
While I watched Mike struggle to put on a pair of pants, I asked, "Can

I help you?" He replied, "No, thank you. I don't want to be a burden." I said, "Helping you is not a burden." He said, "In a couple of months, it might be a burden," I finished, "It will never be a burden."

~

Thank You! I Love You! - December 22, 2017

The morning I got word Randy passed away, I wish someone had first told me to take a seat. I literally dropped to my knees in shock, regret and grief. It was one month to the day after my mom passed away and three days before Christmas.

I hadn't been by to see Randy in a week and a half, and I had the strong urge to drop in the day before just to say hi from afar, as I had been fighting a cold and cough. Busily, I put it off thinking I'd see him in a couple of days to wish him and his family Merry Christmas. Sadly, Randy didn't have a couple of days.

When I first met Randy about nine months before, he was still standing. He leaned up against his chair like Mike did when he could no longer balance well. Although Randy's speech was affected, he was clearly understandable, and I actually found comfort and joy in listening closely to his soft voice. He had that familiar look and sound when he laughed, a wide range of facial expressions, and he got frustrated when he couldn't communicate the way he really wanted to ... classic signs of ALS.

When Erin told me about a friend's dad who had ALS, I thought it was most likely the same man my mom and dad had told me about who lived close to us in our town of Maple Ridge. My parents and Randy and his wife Blanca had a mutual friend, Harry. Harry worked with Randy pre-ALS and was hopeful I would go and befriend the couple. I told my parents I'd gladly go, but didn't want to just show up unannounced. I thought maybe Harry could pass on my contact information or maybe even arrange a visit. As it turned out, I met Randy and his family through Erin, who became instant friends with them when they first met just shortly before she introduced me.

My connection with Randy and Blanca was instant as well. During our first visit, I told them if they needed anything, not to hesitate to email or call. Within days I had a message asking if I knew of any wheelchair vans for rent because they had an appointment in Chilliwack to see the ALS team. I called my friend Cynthia who I knew had a wheelchair van for her dad. Cynthia and family borrowed our wheelchair van when Mike was still alive to take her dad to church on Sundays and on other outings. Cynthia said we could use their van, no problem! I got back to Randy and Blanca and told them I had borrowed a van and then happily offered to drive them. They gratefully accepted.

It was a difficult appointment, for sure. I guess you could say every appointment with the ALS team is difficult because it's about tracking the decline of health and preparing for the next stage of the illness. The ALS team is excellent—they are kind, compassionate and supportive, of course, but that doesn't change the fact that you or your loved one is dying, as there is no cure, no hope of recovering outside of a miracle. Emotions ran high, but by the grace of God we got through it and I felt like the Lord used me and my experience to help in a substantial way. I praised the Lord and lifted my two new friends up to Him in between conversations all the way home.

We had a wonderful visit after the appointment that day, and as I got up to leave I could see Randy had something important he wanted to say. I sat back down and listened closely. We had touched slightly on the topic of faith earlier and he wanted me to know that he wasn't a religious person and that he never went to church. He spoke these exact words: "I wasn't a believer, but now I believe." He explained that God made His existence and His love clear to him through the people he brought into his life, including Erin and me and his dear friend Harry.

It was an unforgettable moment when Randy committed his life to Christ. I prayed and he prayed along with me in his heart, and when we were done he looked up toward heaven and said, "Thank you." It was absolutely beautiful! The three of us, somewhat battered and beaten up by ALS, basked in the power and peace of our Savior's love and His healing touch. At the end of every prayer after that, Randy looked up and said, "Thank you."

There were many more appointments. When I talked to the doctor, respirologist, occupational therapist or whoever, I'd introduced myself as "a friend." Before I could finish, Randy would say "BEST friend!" If Chris or Elanna were along, then he would say "BEST friends!"

There were lots of visits. Sometimes it was just the two of us, like the week I went over every day to sit with Randy when his sister Terri went away. Terri stayed with Randy weekdays when Blanca still worked. Even though Blanca, who worked from home as a child care provider, could keep an ear open and check in on Randy, she really appreciated someone being with him at all times. She and Terri thought I was doing them a favour, but it was the other way around.

Our families became very close and sometimes visits were a little like a party. There was lots of talking and laughing and sharing. There was also a growing sorrow, knowing we were watching another loved one succumb to the dreadful ALS. Every time we said goodbye, Randy proclaimed, "Thank you!" and "I love you!" He said it to everyone individually and we each said it back. When he could no longer say the words, he mouthed them. When he could no longer mouth them, he gave us a certain look that we previously discussed that became his "Thank you!" and "I love you!"

Randy loved massage. Erin usually rubbed his feet and calves. Elanna focused a lot on arms and hands, and I usually stood behind him and rubbed his head, neck and shoulders (not all at the same time, of course).

He was once a man with broad shoulders able to bear the weight of the world: a man's man, good with his hands, a hard-worker, a fisherman and a friend to everyone. I never knew the pre-ALS man with skilled hands, etc. I knew this man who taught himself to operate a motorized wheelchair with his head—extremely determined, sensitive, courageous and vulnerable. He was so caring and kind, a good listener and confidant. A "best friend," indeed.

The regret of not going to see him the day before or a few days before he passed away has often been paralyzing. I've asked God why He didn't make the pull to go over stronger, like He has at other times and many times throughout my life. I've had so much guilt as I questioned, *What kind of best friend was I?* Over the year, God slowly convinced me that I was the best friend I could be to Randy. I don't know the rest, but I have to trust that it was the way it was supposed to be and that it's okay. Plus, Randy would want me to focus on the time we spent together and all the joy we shared, not on the time I wasn't there and the accompanying grief and regret.

Ultimately, we had an extraordinary friendship that changed me forever and I will always treasure.

I know some people were a little concerned about me diving right in with Randy and his family, understandably. Could my heart take the inevitable pain? Could it withstand more breaking? I admit I thought about it too for a few minutes, and then that little bit of doubt was gone. And boy, oh, boy, what I would have missed had I let fear keep me away. That would have been something to really regret!

Randy has left a legacy of faith! As a non-believer, when Randy was diagnosed with ALS he could have become bitter. His attitude could have been, "See, I knew it! Surely, there is no God. And if there is a

God, He's definitely not a good God." Instead, he looked further than that and found the compassionate heart of Jesus. He had little, if any, knowledge of God and no awareness of His love, but in his despair he recognized God was there and that He cared deeply for him with an extravagant, unconditional and eternal love that would never fail him. He looked up and simply said, "Thank you."

At the ALS walk in Abbotsford the spring before Randy died, he had a large team of supporters, mostly people from his work, his family, of course, and mine. Harry was there and I asked Randy if he wanted me to tell Harry that he had a huge influence on Randy's decision to believe and receive Jesus into his life as his Lord and Saviour and ultimate BEST friend. Without hesitation, Randy nodded "Yes!" Randy told me that Harry's constant dedicated walk with the Lord all the years he knew him spoke volumes. He said Harry didn't say much; he just lived out his faith and that other Christian friends made impressions, too.

My mom passing a month before Randy caused me to stuff a lot of my pain away. Writing this piece has forced me to open the door and face some of that grief. It has taken me a few months to get through it and a million tears, but the joy and healing that has come from sorting it out in words and sharing it with you is huge.

Rising out of the ashes: a diamond of a friendship forever in our hearts to be resumed in heaven. We miss Randy so much. He taught us a lot. Our lives will be forever changed because of him.

Dear Randy, thank you! I love you! And Merry Christmas! To Blanca, Terri, Chris and Cory (Randy's boys), thank you for sharing Randy with us!

"Though you have not seen Him, you love Him; and even though you do not see Him now, you believe in Him and are filled with an inexpressible and glorious joy, for you are receiving the end result of your faith, the salvation of your souls."
1 Peter 1:8-9

I wasn't exaggerating the difficulty of writing this piece. I was so heartbroken having to let go of another person to this devastating disease and to watch his family endure such pain. But you can focus on ALS as the enemy (or cancer or any other illness), or you can focus on the Victor and the lessons of love that come from going through it with Him.

Some might say that we were crazy to voluntarily go through that again. But like I said to Blanca recently, "Love always wins." She was telling me, with a huge smile on her face and tears in her eyes, about how she really appreciates the company of her son's dog, but how the backyard now is a real mess because of him. Hence my comment, "Love always wins!" You take the bad with the love.

Of course, there is nothing wrong with protecting yourself and it would have been understandable if I had tried to do so. But I think it was pretty obvious that God wanted me there (us there). He took me there and, of course, He stayed with me, and yes, He allowed me to get crushed. He also showed me new dimensions of His love. Plus, I had already decided I was in it for life—ALS, that is.

It makes me think of Darryl, my "pen PAL" I first told you about in Chapter Ten. PAL, by the way, stands for person with ALS. He's the friend who passed away the same day as my mom. He lived on the other side of the country with his wife and daughters, but I got to meet him in person when he came to stay with his mom and dad for a while about four months before he died.

I guess it was my book that connected us. I gave a copy to my chiropractor, Dr. Brad, to give to his aunt and uncle who are Darryl's parents. Darryl's parents, Carolyn and Derrill, then came to my book signing and got a copy for Darryl. They were so encouraging and just such a lovely couple. Shortly after that, Darryl sent me a message to thank me for my book, and our friendship started right then and there. I got to know him through correspondence on Facebook Messenger.

We talked about a variety of different things—a lot about God, family, Darryl's two trips to Apparition Hill in Medjugorje and the documentary he was in. But he didn't want to burden me with the specifics of his ALS difficulties. He thought I'd probably had more than enough for one lifetime. I assured him that it was okay. I told him that, in part, that's what I was there for. He never really did share much of the hard stuff. He did, however, share a lot about what God was doing in his life in spite of, or maybe I should say, because of the illness.

When I told Darryl about Randy and how we met, he deemed it a "God-incidence" (as opposed to a coincidence). I agreed.

This is the message Darryl sent me after he finished reading my book:

"Hello, Nadine. I'll be honest. I had to put your book down for a bit (your thorough description of one particular day was slightly challenging). Also, after having had a certain level of exposure into your personal life, I wasn't sure I could handle where this story was inevitably headed. But after a couple of days, I decided to get back on my horse of courage and continue reading. I now can say I'm glad I did. The ending was presented in such a way that as a PAL, I was moved by the beauty of it all—love for family, friends, acquaintances, and love for each other, but most importantly, a loving relationship with our Heavenly Father. Thank you for sharing your experiences and teaching me so much. Your PAL, Darryl"

Speaking of "teaching," Darryl couldn't have possibly known what an extraordinary teacher he was to me, a teacher foremost of courage, faith, love and hope. Quite like the other PALS I've known, they all have had a profound gift of teaching. All appointed by God in my life and in the lives of their friends and family to teach and bless and greatly enhance the lives of each one of us.

I finally completed that blog post "Thank You, I Love You" after those grueling months of pouring out my pain over saying goodbye to Randy and the stirring up of sorrow this illness has caused since March 7, 2011. Then I had a thought that totally shocked me. This will be the first time I've shared it with anybody. It kind of went like this—*I wonder when and how I'll meet my next PAL?*

Shortly after that thought, Elanna told me about an old

friend of mine that I had lost touch with. She told me Chuck was staying at her workplace for a week in order for his wife to get some respite. He had already been diagnosed with MS (Multiple Sclerosis) many years back when I knew him from the Rec Centre. I used to visit with him after my fitness classes when he was in the weight room doing his exercises with his trainer, Pamela. I'd sit with him on the stretching table and shoot the breeze—sometimes a light conversation and sometimes deep. I remember following him home one day from the Rec Centre. He explained that the battery on his motorized wheelchair was low and he was afraid he wouldn't make it home. I ended up pushing him part way. We had some great laughs and he thanked me a dozen times. It was my pleasure and that day still brings a smile to my face.

I visited Chuck at Elanna's workplace, and that's when we picked up where we left off. He asked me if I remembered pushing him home. I said I'd never forget. Unfortunately, he had lost most of his ability to speak, so I did most of the talking. Since then, I've visited him during his respite stays (in a couple of places), at the hospital this past summer and fall, and now in hospice.

A few visits ago, he was a little low and I tried really hard to make him smile. He has a smile that lights up a room, and I would have done anything to eliminate the grey space. This is what did the trick—I started talking about our future reunion in heaven and how we are going to have the greatest conversation. I told him we'd sit back and talk about everything he's been trying to tell me. I told him he won't need a push home; he'll walk right in to glory.

Another name to add with Chuck's to the hall of fame

teachers in my life is his wife Beth, his extraordinary caregiver of many years, and more and more my friend.

"Surely Your goodness and unfailing love will pursue me all the days of my life, and I will live in the house of the Lord forever."
Psalm 23:6 (NLT)

CHAPTER 14
Love in Photographs and a First Dance

*"Love never stops loving. It extends beyond the gift of prophecy,
which eventually fades away. It is more enduring than tongues,
which will one day fall silent. Love remains long after words of
knowledge are forgotten."*
1 Corinthians 13:8 (TPT)

I have to admit, there was a lot of chemistry between me and
Chris when we first met. Honestly, I liked it, but at the same
time I didn't. I wasn't supposed to have romantic feelings for
another man yet (or maybe ever). The conversation was silky
smooth; there was never a quiet or awkward moment. There
was laughing and smiling and almost constant eye contact.
About halfway through that three-hour coffee date, I decided I
needed to let him down easy. I needed him to know I belonged
to Another—I certainly didn't need anyone but Jesus. Chris, of
course, knew I was a Christian, but I wanted to make it clear
that Jesus was the love of my life. I thought that might send
him in the other direction. The opposite happened.

Chris explains it like this:

"When Nadine started professing her love for Jesus, in awe,
I held on to that table. I knew right then and there, she was the

answer to my prayers. I had been praying for months leading up to our date, that if there was ever going to be another woman in my life, she'd have a huge heart for Jesus."

Journal entry from April 5, 2016

Chris calls me an answer to his prayers. I call him a ray of sunshine after a very dark cloud finally disappeared. "I keep asking that the God of our Lord Jesus Christ, the glorious Father, may give you the Spirit of wisdom and revelation, so that you may know him better."
Ephesians 1:17 (NIV)

~

When I open the top drawer of my bedside table for a pen or lip balm or anything, what I see first is a picture of me and Mike loosely placed on the top of everything. I open a random book and another picture of us falls out from inside the pages. I have photos and trinkets and little reminders of Mike all over the place.

Love captured in a photograph. Perhaps it sounds like an Ed Sheeran song. Like my dad says his dad always said, "Where have those good days gone?" One day, we'll say the same about these good days. Love never dies … it forever carries on.

When I close the top drawer of my bedside table and turn out the light at night, I am met with Chris' warm embrace. I am held and hugged and enveloped in his love. I sometimes wonder if I'm dreaming even though I know I'm still fully awake. If I wasn't living it, I'd most likely question if this kind of love story could really exist.

If feels like yesterday, and also a lifetime ago. Mike and I were so young, me especially. I guess I thought I knew what I was doing at the age of nineteen; I didn't really know anything. A broken condom led to conception, which led to a short engagement and an elopement. In one moment, the whole course of our lives changed.

It was a rude awakening. It was bumpy in places at times, but we held on tight (like most best friends do) and became a united front (even when we disagreed); we became an excellent team. And then after twenty-six and a half years, so securely tied together, the finish line appeared and ended our three-legged race. Glorious and heart-wrenching in one bittersweet taste.

Since meeting Chris and getting married, I've thought about what others might think. Don't you hate that? When you worry about what others think? It was like I didn't want anyone to assume I had moved on, that my love for Mike had diminished or my grief was gone. As though someone was saying, "Okay, everyone, show's over. There's nothing to see here. Move along." In my writing and in some conversations, I tried to explain. Things have changed—I no longer care what others think. I tell about it now in hopes of encouraging others in their faith. If this love story can renew someone's hope and bring God glory, it's worth all the tears I've cried telling it. Not necessarily a hope to find someone (although that could be), but to find a deeper love connection with Jesus. A hope in unexpected and great things; healing, comfort, the ability to keep moving.

From There to Here in Three Years
- February 22, 2018

I've been calling it "Mike's Flight," but the more I type "Journey of Love," it sounds right too. This one's about naming a painting, remembering Mike, and celebrating life and love in new and wonderful ways.

Leading up to the third anniversary of Mike's passing, I decided I wanted to do something special to express my love, grief and gratitude. Also, with a new year here and the anticipation of turning fifty, I was thinking I should perhaps expand my horizons a little. One way to do both was to paint. I saw a paint night advertised at a local art studio that caught my eye. It was on Friday, January 5 (the anniversary of Mike's passing) and it was a scene of trees, birds and a beautiful sky … it was perfect! Elanna, Chris' sister Kelly, and I went.

Mike has been gone for three years now and it's like a fog recently lifted. I can see beyond my own two feet and the view is exquisite. I just feel so honoured and thankful to have known him, to have called him mine. The gratitude outweighs the grief now, although the grief still weighs a ton sometimes.

Grief has become very intriguing to me. I have found that it changes and weaves and winds in so many ways over time. In his book *A Grief Observed*, C.S. Lewis describes it this way—"Grief is like a long valley, a winding valley where any bend may reveal a totally new landscape." I call it a journey of grief. Also on a journey of love, I explore the great expanse of both. I've come to learn that grief is an expression of love; it's simply a fact of love. In which case, the journey of grief and the journey of love is one.

As most of us know, ALS can be horrible, but here's one way God used it for good: it drove Mike's and my love for each other to heights and widths unmeasurable. I'd have to say our love became perfect. Not that humans can love perfectly, but God does, and His love overtook us. We clung to God and relied on Him exclusively. His love held us up! His love sustained us! His love wooed us and wowed us and the joy we found there couldn't be compared to anything ALS could take from us or anything this world has to offer.

In *A Grief Observed*, Lewis compares the feeling of grief and loss to the feeling of being concussed. I actually had a concussion a few months ago. It was my first and hopefully my last. When I read Lewis' analogy, I thought, *Good one.* He goes on to say, "There is sort of an invisible blanket between the world and me." I can really relate! Recently though, a sort of blanket was lifted. Here's what I mean…

A few weeks ago, Nathan invited me and Chris to a Saturday night church service where he drums sometimes. The music was awesome, and I'm not just saying that because I'm the drummer's mom. It was so powerful! We really felt the heavy presence of God there. About four songs in, they played one of Mike's and my favourite hymns—one we listened to several times during our last few days together called "Lord I Need You" by Matthew Maher. As soon as it started, I closed my eyes and there I was beside Mike in that place of our final goodbye. I've stood there in my mind so many times over these three years, but this time was very different. I've only ever seen the room the way it was, the way I left it—the way I left him. This time, without even a pause from the instant I closed my eyes, it was like a thousand little lights (kind of like fireflies) burst from him in vibrant colours. Dancing, twirling, swirling waves of brilliant energy moved toward the glow of the Lord at the end of the bed. Then came Mike. He leaped out of his body feet first and joined the procession of light. As he pushed off the bed with one arm and reached in the direction he was going with the other, I got a perfect view of his fresh new face and the look of pure elation! I've imagined him moving from his body to the arms of Jesus before, but this was nothing I did. This vision was a gift!

I said earlier "A fog recently lifted," and now I'm thinking maybe I've just climbed above it. Yes, I'm still forgetful, still perimenopausal, still pretty easily distracted. I still feel lost without my mom and miss her something fierce—and so on. The glorious vision I share with you was a wonderful surprise and my painting experience was really cool too, but what has brought me to this exquisite view is simply this: placing one foot in front of the other and keeping my eyes on my Saviour and Guide, Jesus Christ.

Mike and I would have been married for thirty years this June. I think that's pretty incredible! Chris and I will be married for one year in May. I think that's incredible too. Even though our love is young (meaning it hasn't been that long), it's so deep. We didn't really need to test the waters or wade in. We were able to jump right into the deep end. We both knew true love when we saw it and weren't going to let it drift by. It's not always going to be smooth sailing, of course, but I'm overjoyed here in the deep end with Chris. Mike would be thrilled to know how loved and supported and cared for I am. I'd say "I'm lucky in love," but I'm more inclined to use the word "blessed." Chris shows his love and support in so many wonderful ways. He probably has no idea how much even the littlest gesture, like encouraging me to paint a picture for Mike and helping me name it, means to me.

This journey of love I'm on is awesome! The older I get, the more I reflect on the pursuit of God's love for me since day one. His pursuing and wooing has been intense, and the lid of the box I had His love in has long blown off.

One more little story I want to share before I end in hopes of sending you off feeling encouraged and really loved. I've been writing a speech for an upcoming woman's event and before I started preparing, I prayed about it a lot. I felt I had a choice to fall back on the speech I know well—Worrier to Warrior—or wait and listen for something else. At the same time, I was contemplating the new year and the goals I set and some feelings of regret, like I'm falling short in many ways especially as I stare fifty in the face and time keeps slipping through my hands.

I petitioned the Lord in prayer, and one day, right there in the bathtub, I said it again. "Lord, what do You want me to say? What do You want to tell us?"

He replied, "Enjoy my love!"

Then I heard it again with a comma, "Enjoy, my Love."

He calls you and me, Love.

God's beckoning love never ceases to amaze me!

"My response is to get down on my knees before the Father, this magnificent Father who parcels out all heaven and earth. I ask Him to strengthen you by His Spirit—not a brute strength but a glorious inner strength—that Christ will live in you as you open the door and invite Him in. And I ask Him that with both feet planted firmly on love, you'll be able to take in with all followers of Jesus the extravagant dimensions of Christ's love. Reach out and experience the breadth! Test its length! Plumb the depths! Rise to the heights! Live full lives, full in the fullness of God."

Ephesians 3:14-19 (Message)

I had my dad's eightieth birthday on my mind during the time I wrote that last blog post. His birthday was a month after and Elanna and I were planning a big party. She wrote a lovely poem early on and was sitting pretty. It took me a long time. I really wanted it to flow and I struggled to get it right. This is what I came up with—it's not my best work. I could have used more time and I could never say it with the eloquence he deserves, but here goes.

In his forties, instead of buying something sporty like some men in midlife do, our dad sold what he had and headed to the Amazon ... of course, Mom went too.

I recently received a message from a Brazilian friend that read, "My wife and I so dearly love your dad. As you might know, it's because of him that I became a Christian. He witnessed to me as a teenager, and now I am a pastor. From me and my family, Happy Birthday, George!"

This is just one friend among many Dad has led to the Lord.

Dad still travels to Brazil regularly, and somehow ended up in Malawi, Africa about ten years or so ago. At the end of that first visit he said to some women carrying buckets of water on their heads, "I'll be back to drill you a well." He had no idea what he was doing. Concerned, he shared the promise he made with a stranger on the airplane. That stranger happened to be the owner of drilling rigs around that same place. And by God's grace, there are thirty-nine wells to date and six more scheduled for this year!

Here's a few random things you might not know about our dad. He grew up on a farm, the youngest boy in a large family, and sometimes pickings were slim at the end of the dinner table. He says that's why he now spreads the jam real thick on his toast, "Just because I can," he boasts.

Dad loves animals; he still talks fondly of his childhood dogs Teddy and Tommy. He especially loves cats. He picked out my beloved Duffy from the SPCA, and there were others, including a few strays.

Speaking of cats, we think Dad might actually have nine lives. From polio as a kid to pancreatic cancer of late and some other illnesses along the way, his mental strength and perhaps a miracle or two have helped make him the healthy person you see today. Participating regularly in spin classes and walking daily helps too, I'm sure.

Man of Steel could be his nickname because not only did he have amazing pipes (arms), he worked as a metallurgist. He was also a Jack of all trades: carpentry, electricity, landscaping to name a few … I honestly believed and still believe there's nothing he can't do. He continues to travel and run his ministry in these later years.

When it comes to retiring, he says, "I'll play it by ear."

He loved and still loves being "Dad" to us girls and has always wanted to give us the world. Here's a fond memory: when I was about seven or eight, he asked me to go get some groceries from the trunk of his car. There was the bike with the flowered banana seat and high handlebars that I had been admiring earlier that day at the K-mart.

The list of gifts goes on and on… bikes and truck rides, ice cream and tire swings…

He still regularly asks, "Do you need anything?"

Just mention his grandkids or our mom, the love of his life, and watch how his face lights up. His family is his greatest treasure, he's proud as punch and he'd say he's blessed beyond measure.

Today we say thank you for everything, Dad, and Happy 80th Birthday.

We are so proud of you! May God bless you and keep you, and you can be sure that His face will always light up when He talks about you!

I have learned so much more about grief through my dad's experience. That first year after saying goodbye to Mom was a treacherous one, to say the least. There was a lot of reminiscing; childhood memories and forgotten pain was re-emerging. With tears, he shared stories, including detailed accounts of the deaths of his dogs, Teddy and Tommy.

Growing up on a farm in Grunthal, Manitoba, Dad had to develop a thick skin to the death of animals, to extremely hard work, and to a father perhaps not as compassionate when it came to parenting as he would have appreciated. We watched Dad come to terms with some painful father/son relationship situations; lingering sorrow of the passing of four-legged friends and leaving his parents and home for Vancouver, B.C. at the young age of nineteen.

Landing in Port Coquitlam, a little town on the outskirts of Vancouver, wasn't just luck. Of course, it was the brilliant plan of the Lord Himself. Dad met Mom at a dance, but unbeknownst to them both he already knew some of her family; he was rooming and boarding at her cousin's house.

Now, at this stage of his life, having to let go of his beloved wife and having lots of time to think and reminisce, deep wounds and fresh ones were exposed, and we were learning about features of grief and sorrow we had never known.

Dad adored our mom. He honoured the ground she walked on. I wonder if he wonders why he couldn't have gone first as he pines, desperately missing her.

Young couple, Mom and Dad

Dad, if you are reading, thanks for not being afraid to show us your vulnerability; to expose your wounds and let us watch

God soothe them. It's been challenging to observe, but we've witnessed greater measures of God's love and your courage. You and Mom will dance again one day in heaven.

Mom and Dad's 50th wedding anniversary.

I have come to realize that as we age, the journey of grief for most of us can become more arduous. But I also see how the dimensions of God's love expand higher, wider, and deeper as our Heavenly Father takes exceptional care of us.

"He heals the brokenhearted and bandages up their wounds."
Psalm 147:3 (NLT)

Chris and I were relatively young when we became a widow and widower. We are both so grateful to have found each other. But here's a thought that sometimes comes to mind about a future event I dread; having to say goodbye to another husband, or him another wife. I don't want to be a downer, but that's just life. There's this fear that comes with the territory. When I go out or when he leaves the house, I ask myself, *What's the last thing you said?*

Words of advice from a widow and widower—be slow to anger, quick to forgive, say "I love you," and don't leave without a kiss.

Love can break your heart, but it can also fully restore it. It does get easier.

CHAPTER 15
Must Love God and Stepdaughters and Stepsons

*"No, I will not abandon you as orphans—I will come to you. Soon
the world will no longer see me, but you will see me. Since I live,
you also will live."*

John 14:18-19 (NLT)

Leah has an interesting family. It's far from typical and has
experienced a lot of changes over her almost ten years of living.
But one thing is for sure, there is an abundance of love and the
love keeps increasing.

Nathan and his girlfriend at the time, Katrina, were both
eighteen when Leah was born. They got married when Leah
was two, but the marriage didn't last long. Katrina, a few years
later, fell in love with a great guy, Lucas. When these two got
engaged, Leah started calling Lucas, "Stepdad." Katrina and
Lucas produced a beautiful baby boy they named Emerson
(born just days after Mike passed away). Now, Leah had a
brother. And the grandmas and grandpas (Omas and Opas)
were growing in numbers.

My heart was so blessed when Lucas and Katrina asked me
if Emerson could also call me Grandma. "Absolutely!" I said
without hesitation.

Nathan and Lucas became good friends—Nathan says Lucas is just like a brother. Between Katrina and these men, they shared the parenting of the two children. It was neat to see the love and affection Emerson had for Nathan - a second dad, so to speak. Nathan just lived a few doors down, so school and pre-school pickups and drop-offs and other carpooling, sleepovers, pop-ins were their thing.

When Katrina and Lucas broke up, Lucas moved in with Nathan. They quickly realized there wasn't enough room for two, including two children and two dogs, so they moved; the three continued the shared parenting. Fast-forward to today. Lucas and Nathan live in separate places. The three still share parenting and Leah continues to call Lucas her stepdad.

Emerson's recent fourth birthday party was interesting. We laugh when it comes to introductions and the grandparents alone could fill a room. Chris and I were there, along with Katrina's parents and Lucas's parents, including stepparents.

Emerson and Leah

When I met Chris, I learned very fast that he was a stepdad. It didn't take long and he was raving about two beauties. "My girls," he called them. Their situation was unique. These young women, Alexa and Nicola, lost their dad and then a few years later, their mom. It's hard to imagine. I've heard Chris say, with tears in his eyes a few times, "I'm all they've got, and I want to be the best dad I can be for them."

Chris, who came into their lives when they were young teenagers, is their only parent now. Just like most parents, he helps these young adults weather the storms of life, he lends a listening ear and wise advice, he celebrates special occasions and just regular days with them. He's not their parent because he promised Heather he'd always take good care of them (although that is true), but because he loves them like every other mom and dad love their children. To say he adores them is an understatement.

Alexa, Nicola and Nicola's fiancé at the time, now husband Frank, all welcomed me in right away. My children were a little more reluctant when it came to accepting Chris. While they all recognized he was a great guy and were happy I was happy, one of them explained it as a feeling of losing me while still trying to adjust to the recent loss of their dad. It wasn't necessarily too soon for them, it just progressed a little too fast. Now, I'm sure they would agree, they didn't lose me, but instead gained an incredible man into the family.

When I contemplate Alexa and Nicola's situation, I wonder if somewhere inside them, they think it can't get any worse than losing both mom and dad so early in life. Perhaps because of that, they readily accepted me—the potential love and support of another older adult. And of course, someone that made Chris happy.

It didn't take me long at all to fall in love with these three. They are incredible; just lovely. I know the pain cuts extremely deeply sometimes, but there is a joy in them that is contagious. I often wonder how my ears got so lucky to get to take over listening to the beautiful sound of another woman's children's laughter. If Heather was like me, she closed her eyes sometimes and just absorbed the sound of her children laughing.

With these grown ladies in their mid and late twenties, I never really thought of myself as "Stepmom" until one Sunday at church, Nicola introduced us to some friends like this—"My stepdad Chris, and my stepmom Nadine." Nothing she said after "stepmom" registered. I was totally caught off-guard and so honoured. With tears welling, I elbowed Chris and whispered, "Did you hear what she said?"

Alexa, Nicola, Chris and Frank

Whether my children ever introduce Chris as "Stepdad" or not (I have heard one of them refer to him as that and one refer to his girls as stepsisters) it doesn't matter; he loves them like they are his own children. I don't think there is anything he wouldn't do for them. He has jumped at opportunities to help them and I can see he has gained their trust and love more and more. This kind of love—the love of a stepdad or mom—is a very special kind of love. And I am so honoured and blessed to witness the love of many stepparents and to be one.

Wednesdays With Leah - June 24, 2018

June has been an exceptionally busy month, but this past week was a little over the top and I've been feeling physically and emotionally drained. I was pretty tired yesterday when I arrived home after an unusually busy Saturday morning. I went upstairs to have a bath but laid on the bed instead, for just a second. "Just a second" became many seconds. After about ten or fifteen minutes, I remembered I needed to text my sister about something but had left my phone downstairs. Chris gave me his phone to use. While Elanna and I were texting back and forth, a notification came across the screen. It said, "Tomorrow: Nadine and Mike's Anniversary."

I was aware on and off throughout the month that our anniversary was coming up but have a tendency to lose track of the date. When I saw that reminder on Chris' phone, it kind of took my breath away. Even though Chris and I were talking, he had no idea I was all choked up because he was outside in the hall folding laundry.

Thirty years ago today, Mike and I got hitched. I can still see my young self, just a kid oblivious to the journey of love ahead. It feels like yesterday, but at the same time a world away—a world of love, grief, joy, pain and restoration. It's been exceptional, incredible, amazing!

I've just completed Chapter Five of my next book. I'm not under the same pressure to get it done as I was with the first one, so it's slower going than I'd like. I need to be more disciplined with my time. Having said that, though, I put it on hold while I write this piece. I look at this as a little reprieve and an opportunity to connect with whoever takes the time to read it.

This new book, like the first one, includes my blog posts. I don't have as many this time, so there will be more fresh writing. This book also includes some journal entries from the journal I kept when Mike was first diagnosed with ALS. I treasure that journal, of course, but reading it isn't easy and I've had to be more vulnerable than ever sharing some of it. I always envisioned me reading it to Mike years later, dreaming he'd either be healed of ALS or long outlive the statistics.

Something I'm noticing as I go through that journal is the regular (maybe monthly) sleepovers with Leah. Here's mention of a couple:

Journal entry from July 22, 2011

When Nathan dropped Leah off, Elanna was over. We all went for a walk. Leah slept between me and Mike. I just love watching her sleep...

Journal entry from July 23, 2011

I awoke early and got up, leaving Leah and Mike in bed. I read and prayed for a while, and then Mike came down and joined me. Leah followed shortly after. We had the usual for breakfast—smoothies. We sat on the front porch and listened to the birds and played with our dog, Molly.

~

Leah was two at the time. She is nine now, and throughout this school year she's had regular overnight stays on Wednesdays. She has stayed other nights a few times as well, which is a bonus, sometimes with Emerson, which is another bonus. But Wednesdays are our nights.

Chris picks Leah up from school on Wednesday afternoons and I meet them at our place shortly after— when I arrive home from work. She spends time on my iPad. She loves to make movies, play games and watch videos (she and Chris enjoy the funny cat/dog videos, I enjoy the laughter). We have painted on numerous occasions, watching YouTube tutorials as well as directive drawings. We go for walks with the dog(s) and sometimes to the playground at the school down the road or in our complex. She's teaching me to crochet—that's what we did last week. We have gone a few times to visit the residents where Elanna works and Leo and Glen (our "therapy" dogs) volunteer. And we almost always go for dinner with my dad to Tim Hortons. Bedtime is lovely. She usually plays a little more on the iPad while I get ready. Then we read a book, say our prayers and say goodnight. Sometimes while she drifts off to sleep, I sit up beside her and read or write.

I know I am lucky. I know I am incredibly blessed. I don't take this time for granted. Wednesdays with Leah are a gift!

We still have the "usual" for breakfast and Chris typically takes her to school while I get ready for work, but sometimes I take her, too. A couple of weeks ago when I dropped her off, as soon as I said, "Goodbye, I love you!" I thought to myself, *Soon she'll be graduating from high school.* It goes so fast. I felt sad. Michaela was graduating that weekend, so maybe that's why I had that thought. Luke is one year behind her. I occasionally picked Michaela and Luke up from elementary school when Elanna worked, and now they are almost all grown up. I say to myself what I said when my children graduated, *You shouldn't have blinked.*

When I dropped Leah off and had that split-second graduation thought, I asked myself if I was savouring every moment, unlike with my own children. Time seemed to slip right though my fingers. I'm not as busy now, and I'm wiser; I know better than ever how time flies.

Along with Michaela's graduation, June included birthdays, the ALS walk, a few friends' book launches, many appointments for my ongoing whiplash injury, a memorial service, a bridal shower for my Auntie Marguerite, and the list goes on.

But then everything came to a halt. Last week after a class I was teaching, I received word that Bruce, my cousin Shelley's husband, had passed away that morning from a heart attack. And the whirlwind stops for a while as you try to wrap your head around that one. As Elanna and I made our way over to Shelley's place, we wondered if at this stage of life, what's the rest going to be be like: trying to comfort each other in our losses, illnesses, grief, shock? That was last Wednesday (June 20).

Just two days before that, on Monday, while I was at work, I had a 911 voice mail from a good friend. She asked if there was any way I could go sit with her son, who was having emergency surgery that day. She was out of town and couldn't get there until much later. He had got himself to the hospital just in time. He almost died.

There are constant reminders that life is so fragile, and that tomorrow is not a given. Today is to be embraced and savoured. Some get more time than they expect, like Karen's dad who outlived his prognosis by a year. Then there's Bruce; he was young, three boys still at home, no warning and he's gone. Shelley's mom, Auntie Vicki, greets us at the door and tells us there's just one question on her mind—"Why?"

We all ask why from time to time. Lots of things just don't seem right ... things don't always make sense. I find the older I get and the more knowledge and wisdom I gain, the less knowledgeable and wise I am ... about life, about God, about everything. The mysteries are bigger, but you know what? So is God!

"Indeed these are the mere edges of His ways, and how small a whisper we hear of Him! But the thunder of His power who can understand?"

Job 26:14 (NKJV)

This past Wednesday, we went to McDonald's for dinner instead of Tim's. Dad had a gift card he wanted to use, plus Tim's has been out of chili a few too many times lately. Leah brought a card for her great-granddad that she made at school. It was a thank you card with lovely words, a drawing of a horse and a loonie (one-dollar coin) she found, taped to the inside. He loved it! What a beautiful scene it was, the two of them sitting side by side with the homemade card proudly displayed on the table in front of them. He kept offering her his fries (even though she had her own) and his drink. He also slipped her a little cash in there at some point. The thing is, he'd give her the world if he could. But here's another thing, he's giving her more than that. He's giving her his time and attention. He's telling her stories and imparting wisdom. He's speaking to her words of praise and encouragement. He's sharing his food, money, his life, his love. My dad who recently turned eighty with his precious great-granddaughter, sharing food at McDonald's, was the most beautiful sight to behold. Not everyone gets that kind of gift and I know they know it, especially him.

Dad and Leah

Today (June 29), our dogs Leo, Glen and I had so much fun at Elanna's work, going around and visiting the residents with her. Elanna eventually had to get back to her routine and went on her way. I told her that before we left, we'd have one last visit with our friend Jean. Jean is always so happy to see us. She loves to sing, and while Glen sat on her tummy and Leo at the end of her bed, she sang a few songs for us. I asked her if she knew the song "Jean" from the movie *The Prime of Miss Jean Brodie* (1969). I explained it was my late husband Mike's favourite song and we listened to it often. She wasn't sure, so I found it on YouTube and played it for her. We sang along a little. She asked me to print out the lyrics and bring them next time. I said I would. She asked me to also bring the lyrics to "Moon River." I responded, "Wow Jean, Mike and I loved that song and we also listened to that one a lot." I told her I'd bring the lyrics for both songs next time. She thanked me for coming and commented that it was the best visit. I agreed. She didn't need a thing from me; just a little bit of my time was the greatest gift she could receive … and I treasure her time as well!

After Chris wished me a happy anniversary last Sunday, he went off to church. He was on PowerPoint and had to leave early. I went to Nathan's church to hear him drum. It was unusual that I beat Chris home. Soon after, though, he came through the door with two lovely bouquets of flowers. He handed me one, gorgeous with brilliant colours, and said, "These are from Mike." He handed me another, smaller bouquet of daisies, and said, "These are from me." Later, he informed me that he knew I liked daisies and that those daisies might not be real daisies, but they looked like daisies and, well, the price was to his liking. I replied, "Oh, so that's why the more extravagant ones are from Mike?" He responded, "Yeah!" Then after a pause, he continued, "Do you think it's possible to get reimbursed?" We both laughed. Mike would probably say, "It's okay, I'll give her the daisies."

Not everyone gets this kind of gift and we both know it! I will hold on to it for as long as I can and do my best to savour every moment!

"Collect moments not things. Treasure time together. Value love above all else. Be grateful."
Happy Wives Club.com

To my dear cousin Shelley and your boys, and Auntie Vicki and cousin Larry, I am so sorry for your loss. You are in my prayers and thoughts. Bruce was an exceptional man! I end with a few lessons we could all learn from him: Be exceedingly kind and give generously of your time. Lend a helping hand as much as you can. Pour yourself out!

Just a warning for this next one: your face might get wet from crying and sore from smiling...

Must Love Long Walks and God - September 3, 2018

As much as I absolutely hate saying goodbye to summer, I'm getting excited to welcome fall. I can hear its faint whisper just around the corner. It's already preparing us for its arrival with its intermittent cool breezes and changing leaves. In only a matter of time those autumn colours will speak, "Maestro, music please."

Another summer has flown by. I predicted it back in June when co-workers were counting down the days to summer holidays. In my head I was thinking, *Please don't.* As quickly as it comes, it goes. I am ultra-aware of time's ability to fly by, to pass even quicker than last year. So I try with all my might to embrace each day, every hour and minute for what it is—a gift!

Speaking of gifts and how time flies, my fiftieth birthday recently came and went ... obviously, I survived! Letting go of my forties was like letting go of other things I've come to love; I grieved giving them up, but I happily keep marching on. It felt like a bit of an accomplishment actually, but more so, I was just so grateful and humbled to reach this milestone.

Among the many highlights of the summer, turning the big 5-0 was one and taking Leah horseback riding almost weekly was another. Then there's this one—the one this blog post is based on: my aunt's wedding. Ultimately, the highlight is the incredible love story. So, I'll go back to the beginning. Or at least back to when we first started noticing something was happening.

Auntie Marguerite is one of the most jovial people I know. Good cheer, laughter and smiling are her specialties. It kind of runs in the family. She is my mom's younger sister and they are so similar in this way. Anyway, to see her typically large smile increase gave us a clue something was up.

She shared with us that she had started walking on a regular basis. She actually found a walking partner, a nice man from her church. Over the course of about eight months, every time we saw her there was an indication that maybe this male walking partner was becoming more than just a friend. After a visit with her, I'd say to my sister, "Did you see that ear-to-ear grin?" After another visit, Elanna would say, "Did you see her nails were done?" And of course, she was looking extremely fit. The frequency and distance of their walks was increasing.

One day, Auntie M confessed that she had developed some romantic feelings for this lovely Frenchman, Jean-Marc (or John, as she called him). She was concerned though, that the feelings weren't mutual. She said that she was making her hand available for holding but he wasn't noticing. She said he talked a lot about his late wife, which she really liked, but thought maybe he wasn't ready yet.

Then, one day I got the long awaited call from my ecstatic Auntie Marguerite announcing that Jean had professed his love for her. She said what he said was absolutely beautiful and took her by complete surprise. I think it was about the one-year mark from when they started their walking partnership.

Their wedding was just a couple of weeks ago. It was an emotional occasion, to say the least. Auntie Marguerite, who recently turned seventy, had been a widow for forty years. And Jean-Marc, seventy-five, had been a widower for ten. I think these two probably never imagined that God had such extravagant plans for them at this stage of life. It's a love story I'm sure the Lord is using to prove how He doesn't stop moving mountains in our lives. Time doesn't matter to Him. It doesn't stop Him from renewing hope in a defeated soul, or providing a friend, husband or wife, or answering a prayer we've given up on, or shaping us into the glorious likeness of His Son.

Anyway, I don't think I've missed my mom as much as I did the week of my aunt's wedding. It's funny because, at the same time, I was writing Chapter

Twelve in my next book, which is all about my mom. I was just telling how my mom would light up when she talked about how excited she got on payday to buy her brothers and sister new clothing; how she loved dressing her little sister up and doing her hair. Aunty M still talks about how my mom (eleven years older than her) doted on her and spoiled her and how it blessed her beyond measure.

The week leading up to the wedding, Elanna and I helped our aunt find the perfect white fascinator to wear and someone to do her hair. It wasn't until after that I thought, that's what our mom would have done ... she'd be so happy we helped take care of those details, in particular.

Elanna and I went to Auntie M's house early in the morning the day of the wedding. We wanted to be there to make some introductions when Jackie, our hairstylist and friend, arrived. Aunty Marguerite was as giddy as a schoolgirl and on cloud nine ... just so excited! I was sad in a way because my mom would have been there having so much fun, but I was also as happy as I've ever been for anyone.

Our aunt and Jackie hit it off right away, like we knew they would. Auntie M proceeded to tell Jackie, through the permanent smile on her face, all about her wonderful fiancé. I don't think she could have stopped talking if she wanted to and Jackie happily listened as she blow-dried and brushed, curled and sprayed.

Earlier, my aunt asked her daughter Colleen to fix up a bouquet of not-so-fresh flowers on her dining room table. Colleen and her sister-in-law Shalin were busy doing their daughters' hair and Colleen told her mom that those flowers didn't really matter right then and she'd do it later. So when I had a minute, I took the vase of flowers into the kitchen to clean them up, and this is where everything kind of stopped for one very profound moment. Alone there, freshening up the week-old bouquet of flowers, I could hear Auntie M say, "Have I told you about my husband who passed away?" Just typing this sentence opens up the floodgates.

I can't stop thinking about this moment. It was almost like God was saying to me, "Nadine, you will never stop telling people about your husband who passed away either. You will go on about Mike and love him for the rest of your life. At the same time, you will be on cloud nine for a long time about marrying Chris and you will continue to fall deeper and deeper in love with him."

So, needless to say, the waterworks were just getting started and we hadn't even gotten to the church yet.

The ceremony was lovely and I pretty much held it together until the reception. We sat at what I called the "cool" table with Auntie Vicki and cousins Shelley and Larry. We had lots of fun and I just kept thinking how brave Shelley was and how she must still be in shock, having recently lost her husband Bruce so suddenly. At a celebration like this, I'm sure she'd feel so lost there without him.

After dinner and before the speeches, I went over to the equally-as-"cool" table beside us where Auntie Gail, Uncle Larry and cousins Julie and Chrissy were sitting to say hello. Uncle Larry jokingly said to me (I think he was joking), "Our table took a vote and we nominate you to speak at the open mic on our behalf." This started a little back and forth about why the other was the better choice to get up there and say something.

I really wish I could have risen to the occasion, but I'm just not good on the spot. Plus, I was so emotional. Had I taken that microphone and opened my mouth, a bunch of blubbering would have come out and that wouldn't have been "cool" at all.

If I had more time to think about it and been able to keep my cool, I probably would have simply started by introducing us—the children of Auntie Marguerite's siblings Uncle Larry and the two in heaven, my mom and Uncle Eugene. Without conferring with my cousins, I know I could have said that to each of us, Auntie M simply represents love. Even though she raised four children of her own and has many grandchildren, a few great grandchildren, and lots of friends and family, when she is with any of us, we receive her undivided attention and buckets of love. She genuinely cares deeply for each of us. It's a selfless love that spreads beyond limits. Her role-modelling of love has been exquisite!

She loves God first, and then the person right in front of her (regardless of who it is), and all the people around her. And now, Jean-Marc, this very blessed Frenchman, moves up the queue and gets the best view of this incredible love in action. The more I get to know him, the more I realize it's well deserved, and Auntie M is also very blessed to get a similar, very special, exquisite love in return. And we all wish them many wonderful years of marital bliss, good health and happiness!

So, it's taken me about a week to write this and we're that much closer to fall. School starts tomorrow, and that's when I go back to work. I partly chose this career as an education assistant because of the awesome holidays, but as hard as it is to let go of the freedom of summer, I'm ready for routine and I'm ready to see those beautiful children's faces.

What I hope to take with me to work and everywhere I go, is more love—this exquisite love from above that spreads beyond limits—and greater expectations in God. Remember that anything is possible with Him!

"Now to Him who is able to do exceedingly abundantly above all that we ask or think, according to the power that works in us, to Him be glory..."
Ephesians 3:20

After Auntie Marguerite and Jean's wedding ceremony, my cousin Ryan, her third child of four who was sitting right in front of us, turned around and with a big smile proclaimed, "I guess I finally have a stepdad."

"Father to the fatherless, defender of widows—this is God, whose dwelling is holy. God places the lonely in families; He sets the prisoners free and gives them joy."
Psalm 68:5-6 (NLT)

CHAPTER 16
Good News of Great Joy and My Love for Squats and Lunges

"Scripture reassures us, 'No one who trusts God like this—heart and soul—will ever regret it.'"
Romans 10:13 (Message)

If the news is on, I usually leave the room or I'll ask Chris, "Can we change this?" My thought: ignorance is bliss. Not exactly. It's important to know what's going on in the world, but to watch the news without a certainty of the sovereignty of God is extremely daunting and depressing, to say the least. Even with a strong faith in God, it can still be those things. But with eyes on Him, there's peace in these troubled waters—in the constant bombarding of terrible news.

Don't you just love good news? I think the human race is starving for good news. When we hear a good news story, it's like we all get up and cheer. "Yay! Good news! We love you! Where have you been? Come again soon!"

There is a certain Good News that accompanies us in the trenches of grief. There is Good News that never leaves us, that retrieves us, that frees us, that grants us faith to increase our belief and helps us with our unbelief. It enables us to keep going and to keep hoping and to keep looking up...

Good News of Great Joy - November 30, 2018

Lately, I've had a word stuck in my head. It's nothing unusual - I'm often contemplating a word or a message of some sort. Out of the blue, it just appears on my plate—something for me to chew on. It can be a Bible verse, a quote or just a persistent thought. It can last for days, weeks, even months.

For instance, for quite a while this year it was all about the fruit of the Spirit from Galatians 5:22-23. I already knew that verse well. I can rattle off those fruits no problem: Love, joy, peace, patience, kindness, goodness, faithfulness, gentleness and self-control. See, no problem. I know them all and don't even have to look.

But the question I kept getting was, *Do you really know them? Do you know them deeply? Are you living them out? Are you walking in step with the Spirit? Does He have His way in you?* The proof is in these attributes.

Then I find myself on a quest: comparing translations, contemplating each word, researching and searching my heart, and asking God to search me and to show me what He finds. Then He shows me in a number of different scenarios, often in traffic when I'm stuck behind someone going really slowly or when I have to stop for every light—and I realize I still have a long way to go in honing those attributes. It's one thing to be able to rattle off some words in your sleep and a whole other thing to live them out every waking moment of the week.

As much as I still contemplate the fruit of the Spirit,

I've had other words since then. Recently, it's the word "intention." As I study the word "intention" though, I wonder if the word "purpose" is more apropos.

For example, I'm totally stuck on Chapter Thirteen of the book I'm writing. I'm stuck there for a few reasons: straight up procrastination, it's hard work, it can be painful at times, and I'm busy doing other things. While I've been busy doing other things, I've been asking myself what my intentions are ... or purpose. I ask myself why I am writing this book. Am I doing it to be praised, for esteem? Or am I doing it to obey and glorify Him? It's definitely not for the money. FYI: publishing a book actually costs a lot of money and the probability of making it big in this industry is less likely than being struck by lightning.

Writing this book might be a good idea, but is it a God idea? I'm asking myself and God that about everything lately. I just want to be fulfilling His plans. Although I know I don't get it right all the time, I do rely on Him to guide me. My heart's desire is to stay in step with Him—to abide. I sometimes call it being in the "bullseye." There are roads paved with good intentions, and then there are those paved with God intentions. The latter is the road that leads to His joy, contentment and peace ... and, of course, obeying them is key.

Another word of late has been "listen." With "listen" comes slow down, be quiet, stop for a minute.

One morning a couple of weeks ago, I got up feeling low, like dread had entered without knocking.

I had been injured at work a few days before, which exacerbated the injury from last year. I know, this education assistant job sounds dangerous, doesn't it? It can be. Plus, my job situation was changing and I had a big decision to make (in hindsight, it wasn't that big, but for a few days, it felt huge). But much more than all that, I had two friends on my mind, one in hospice and the other recently home from the hospital, very ill and fighting with all her might, hoping for a miracle.

I came downstairs to let Leo out for a pee and get things started. I stopped, stood still for a minute and had a little conversation with my soul. I know. Weird, right? Have you ever had words with your soul? Mine went something like this. "Oh my soul, why are you so low? Don't lose hope, don't lose hope! Just praise the Lord, soul. There are a million things to praise Him for."

A wooden sign that says "Be Hopeful" caught my eye. It's a sign I usually have elsewhere but put there a week earlier when I was decorating for the birthday party we had for this fighter friend I mentioned— Shonia (pronounced Shauna). Then I thought to check my Bible app for the verse of the day (I usually check it before I get out of bed). This is what it said:

"Why, my soul, are you downcast? Why so disturbed within me? Put your hope in God, for I will yet praise Him, my Saviour and my God."

Psalm 42:5 (NIV)

I thought, *Wow! That sounds very familiar.* God heard me and showed me I'm not alone. The Psalmist and all of us are in the same boat, sometimes just trying to stay afloat, hoping our souls respond to the occasional lament/pep talk. I didn't necessarily feel that much better, but a strong reminder that God knows all about it brought some relief.

I just kept thinking of Shonia in so many ways. 1) Does it bring her relief that God knows all about it when she's injecting a handful of needles every three hours into the only flesh left on the tops of her legs; 2) How futile my little troubles are in light of Shonia's battle and how humbling it is knowing God cares about both; and, 3) Could Shonia have any idea how her true grit and persistence have been a huge source of inspiration to me and so many of us? Elanna and I discuss it after every visit. We are always like, "Wow, she's amazing!"

All the tests, all the needles, the surgeries, ports, tubes, chemo, hospital stays, procedures, exhaustion, nausea, pain, dashed dreams, the pleas for mercy and healing—I'm sure Shonia could add many more words to this list, but I think we all get the drift.

We are flabbergasted by her strength and determination, her staying power, how she's done some trips of late having to find in advance a nearby hospital for weekly intravenous. Most of us would have thrown in the towel by now. Instead, Shonia goes away for the weekend with a friend, even though she has to get up every three hours to administer her meds. As much as possible, she's not letting it stop her from living her life to the fullest. What she's been through is unimaginable for most, but she just keeps going—showing us what perseverance, a positive attitude and faith can do.

Faith. Now there's an encouraging word. It means nothing, though, if not exercised. Regarding Shonia's cancer, I sometimes think it's just too big. But then I say, "Come on, faith, let's go! Get those knees up. There's always hope! With God, all things are possible; He is a God of endless resources—of countless miracles!" Shonia says she received a miracle regarding her health many years ago (her case is actually cited in a medical journal), and she is confident she could be granted one again.

Our word for Shonia is "hope." Another is "good news." During her last hospital stay, there came a day where the bad news was all-consuming. Looking a little defeated, when asked how we could pray, she said she could really use some good news. Over the course of the next few days, as I prayed for just a sliver, just even a glimmer of good news, I kept thinking about the everlasting, never changing, Good News—Jesus Christ.

With the Christmas season now upon us and this talk of Good News, I hear the little voice of Linus Van Pelt responding to Charlie Brown's bemoan, "Does anyone know what Christmas is all about?" Linus recites Luke 2:8-12, part of which says, "And the angel said unto them, Fear not: for, behold, I bring you good news of great joy, which shall be to all people. For unto you is born this day in the city of David a Saviour, which is Christ the Lord…"

Well, I've finally finished Chapter Thirteen. It's such a relief. Even though this book is taking so long, I try to focus on how far I've come. Way back in Chapter Two, I wrote all about "hope." Hope was the word Mike and I got a lot and chewed on and pondered and embraced throughout our toughest days. It's still one of my favourites.

In that hope chapter, I explain that even though I still (of course) hope for a cure for ALS and healing for other illnesses and many things, my hope is so much more than an expectation in something; it's a confident expectation and assured certainty in Someone.

So let us take this from the Psalmist: Put your hope in God and praise Him!

From Linus and the apostle Luke: Fear not, Good News of great joy was born—a Saviour, which is Jesus. That's what Christmas is all about.

From Shonia: Live every day to the fullest. Never give up. Believe in the power of prayer and the possibility of a miracle!

From me (from the first verse I memorized): Trust in the Lord with all your heart, and do not lean on your own understanding. In all your ways acknowledge Him, and He will direct your paths. Proverbs 3:5-6

Like Chapter Thirteen, this blog post has taken me a while. My dad and Chris were in Malawi, Africa when I started it, and have since returned having had three more wells drilled there. That is forty-four wells now under Project Wellness' belt. Chris and Dad were so honoured to have our local Member of Parliament, Dan Ruimy, and his assistant Khalida along with them. Dan and Khalida said it was a lot of fun and hope to join them again sometime. I'm getting a little antsy to go soon again myself. This full-blown fear of flying hinders me but I'm sure if it's God's will, He'll enable me.

I end with a verse my dad quoted the other day. He said it was one of the first he committed to memory. Considering my writing and missionary work at home and possibly abroad, this verse spoke to me. It's a verse for all of us to ponder. Let's chew on this: "I pray that you may be active in sharing your faith, so that you will have a full understanding of every good thing we have in Christ." Philemon 1:6

P.S. Elanna and I went for dinner with Shonia tonight and we had a very nice time. It's a humbling and lifting experience being in her presence. Elanna and I walked away like always, amazed … and I say to my soul, "Stay hopeful and praise God!"

"Come on faith, let's go! Get those knees up. There's always hope! With God all things are possible; He is a God of endless resources—of countless miracles!" I guess this statement in that Good News of Great Joy piece came from the fitness instructor in me. "Let's go. Get your knees up!" Exercising faith is vital to the soul just as exercising the body is to the heart, lungs and muscles.

I've always enjoyed being physically active. As far back as I can remember, I've liked moving my body. I played a variety of sports as a kid and teenager and was a decent athlete—coordinated and quite fast. I started attending group fitness classes when I was about sixteen. I did that on and off until I gave birth to Erin when I was twenty. After that, I became a regular and never looked back.

As a new mom without a career or any career aspirations, despite some fear and self-doubt, but with a lot of support from my encouraging spouse, I decided to become a fitness instructor. I was so close to walking away that day when I went to register for the course. If Mike hadn't accompanied me, I'm sure I would have. I am so grateful for Mike's confidence in me and God's courage and strength. And to tell you the truth, it wasn't difficult for me. Teaching fitness classes came very naturally. Over the years, it's become like breathing.

In 1990, I was newly certified as a fitness instructor and pregnant with Nathan. I was proud to teach right up until a few days before I gave birth to him. With two babies eighteen months apart, I had this incredible outlet. I was officially a working mother of two, taking total ownership of this part-time job with obvious health benefits and (in most cases) child-minding.

I entered the industry right when professional aerobics music and the Step was being introduced. I signed up for a workshop called Bench Works, having no idea what I was getting into. It was my first time on the Step. The extremely energetic, super friendly, muscly fitness presenter had the huge crowd going in every direction—on, over and across the step. I left with a massive headache and on cloud nine. That's the day I officially fell in love with step aerobics. I convinced the woman I worked for at the time to purchase some steps. She reluctantly did, wondering where on earth she was going to store this clumsy apparatus. I assured her we'd make it work.

Step aerobics was huge! Not as big today, but the step is still used and my love for it continues. I incorporate it into my classes regularly. I have spent an uncountable amount of hours over the years experimenting with patterns and different exercises, finding a host of moves that amazed myself and others. I even dreamt about the step sometimes. I don't discriminate, though; I like other equipment and most types of classes.

At the age of twenty-five (in 1994), with six-month-old Madison in my arms, I opened the doors for the first time to Fitness Works, the studio Colleen and I started. That is quite a significant memory, for sure. In my thirty years of teaching group fitness, I co-owned and operated that facility for five years, managed the group fitness program at the Recreation Centre here in Maple Ridge where I still work, and the Recreation Centre in our neighbouring town of Pitt Meadows. I became Heart and Soul Fitness Ltd. and taught at numerous gyms, have taken probably a hundred-plus workshops, and also led some. I trained others to teach and I've done a fair share of mentoring. I have taken kinesiology and personal training courses, to name a few, and have held multiple certifications. I feel I've come full circle, as now I just enjoy teaching a couple of classes a week. I am so grateful for a healthy, strong body and the ability to continue to do what I love with all my heart and soul.

Like anything, there are pros and cons. Some of the pitfalls have been exhaustion, a few (mostly minor) injuries, negotiating for more money, and having to sub classes unexpectedly when an instructor was sick or just wanted to spend time with her/his family. The pros far outweigh the cons, though: making friends is number one (some of my colleagues and participants have become lifelong friends), free gym memberships, a creative outlet, and sometimes a ministry. Here is a perk I've realized exceedingly more over the years—it's been an anti-depressant. I have said before, it has saved me.

When Mike suspected he had ALS, we were both a mess. I think those few weeks leading up to his diagnosis was the worst part of the whole illness ... maybe not, but the anticipation was excruciating. I remember teaching my classes and being totally pre-occupied. I was leading thirty-plus people through some fairly complicated step choreography and in a completely different world inside. Turning on a big smile when you are sick or sad is par for the course but enlisting the auto pilot in this situation was downright unsafe, and I knew it. I also knew I'd go insane without it. And that's how I felt many times throughout Mike's illness and on other occasions as well.

I've told Chris if I'm ever going out of my mind or if I'm looking down and dragging my butt around, get me to the gym (and, of course, pray for me too). I think in this day and age, it's common knowledge that exercise has huge physical and mental health benefits. God has used exercise in my life many times to get me out of bed, to straighten out my head, to fill me with purpose, to pour out His love through people and endorphins, to help me glorify Him and worship ... and on goes the list.

I know my love for fitness has been evident to those around me. I assume it's a big part of the reason why both of my daughters also became fitness instructors. I hope that my love for God and my strong faith in Him is even more evident. I say that fitness has saved me, but I don't put my faith in fitness; I put it in God. Fitness has been a huge blessing. It has helped me immensely and I'm so thankful for its numerous benefits, but exercising my faith has been a higher priority. Leading a group of people through an interval workout using the step and weights might be my specialty but I desire mostly that God sees my faith and is pleased. Hebrews 11:6 says, "Without faith, it is impossible to please God..."

I've been contemplating that verse for a while now, having recently gone through a bit of a trial ... I'd call it a testing of my faith. I've been asking myself questions like, *How much do you really love the Lord? Are you trusting in Him with all of your heart? Is your faith pleasing God?* I'm often at odds with my sinful self and this kind of questioning isn't that unusual. But then He, so full of grace and mercy, does something to reveal to me that I am deeply in love and completely devoted to Jesus. I'm never going to be perfect (in this human body) or even close, and I'm frequently convicted of something and feeling remorseful, but the good news is, my sin has been bought and paid for in full. And the longer I follow Jesus, the stronger my faith and the deeper my love for Him grows.

God really spoke to me recently when I was in one of those remorseful, questioning modes. While Chris was driving and I was reading aloud Oswald's devotion of the day, I was met there in the passenger seat again with His mercy and grace.

The teaching is taken from John 21:15-17. Jesus and Peter are talking (this is after Jesus' resurrection) and Jesus asks Peter three times if he loves Him. Peter says yes every time. It tells us that Peter is hurt when Jesus asks him that third time and Peter responds, "Lord, you know all things; you know that I love you."

Why would Jesus ask this question when He already knew Peter's heart? This disciple and good friend denied Jesus three times leading up to His crucifixion, and the way Oswald sees it, Jesus wanted Peter to believe in the depths of his being that he loved his Lord beyond a shadow of a doubt, despite failing Him and despite his imperfections. That's good news for me and you.

This is what Oswald says:

"Peter was grieved because He said to him the third time, 'Do you love Me?' Yet he was awakened to the fact that at the centre of his personal life he was devoted to Jesus. And then he began to see what Jesus' patient questioning meant. There was not the slightest bit of doubt left in Peter's mind; he could never be deceived again. It was a revelation to him to realize how much he did love the Lord, and with amazement he simply said, 'Lord, You know all things.'

"Peter began to see how very much he did love Jesus, and there was no need to say, 'Look at this or that as proof of my love.' Peter was beginning to discover within himself just how much he really did love the Lord. He discovered that his eyes were so fixed on Jesus Christ that he saw no one else in heaven above or on the earth below. But he did not know it until the probing, hurting questions of the Lord were asked…

"Oh, the wonder of the patient directness and skill of Jesus Christ with Peter! Our Lord never asks questions until the perfect time. Rarely, but probably once in each of our lives,

He will back us into a corner where He will hurt us with His piercing questions. Then we will realize that we do love Him far more deeply than our words can ever say."

Oh, how special the relationship between Jesus and Peter—an exquisite display of faithfulness and love and an example for all of us. I have this picture in my mind of Peter climbing out of the boat during that raging storm, so eager to meet Jesus walking on the water toward him and the other disciples. Who would even think of it? Peter calls out to Jesus, "If it's You, tell me to come to You on the water." (Matthew 14:28). Only a man or woman so enamoured with someone and so entirely fixed on Him could forget the fierce waves. Jesus calls back, "Come!" (Matthew 14:29) With reckless abandon, Peter gets out of the boat. It's like he forgets about the storm and that it's humanly impossible to walk on water. It reminds me of that vision I had of Mike when he leaped out of his body toward the light of Jesus at the end of his deathbed. Peter's focus on Jesus erases his fear, but a few wet steps in, Peter sinks.

How many of us have been there? So focused on Him we forget what is impossible for a human, and then we take our gaze away and a few wet steps in, we start to sink. Matthew 14:30 says, "But when he saw the wind, he was afraid and, beginning to sink, cried out, 'Lord, save me!'"

This next verse is where most of our attention should go—on the saving power, compassion and love of Jesus. "Immediately, Jesus reached out His hand and caught him." Peter would have drowned—we would all drown—if it wasn't for His strong hand. Then Jesus says to Peter, "You of little faith, why did you doubt?" (Matthew 14:31) Wow, I think it's so interesting that Peter, as far as we know, is the only person to have ever walked on water, and instead of congratulating him on accomplishing the impossible, Jesus asks, "Why did you doubt?"

Peter obviously had notable faith, incredible focus and a deep love for Jesus to be able to forget the chaos, hop out of that boat and walk on water. Also, there is no mention of any of the other disciples following suit. So why did Jesus say what He did? I think maybe it's because, like Peter said when Jesus was questioning him about his love, "Lord, you know all things…" Jesus knew that Peter, like every other human being, struggled with doubt, especially when the storms of life arose. Jesus would have seen the potential—the faith, the focus, the love and devotion—and knew that Peter, when fully trusting in Him, was capable of walking further on that water than he ever could have imagined. I can't see why it would be different for any of us.

"There are three of you. There is the person you think you are. There is the person others think you are. There is the person God knows you are and can be through Christ."
Billy Graham

His name was Simon and Jesus calls him Peter, which means "rock." He was a fisherman turned fisher-of-men; sometimes impulsive, often outspoken, totally flawed … but chosen. A regular man, humbled, broken and rescued; saved by God's grace, a proclaimer of the Good News; an example for me and you.

Our faith grows and becomes stronger over time just as our bodies become fitter with consistent exercise but here is some encouragement for the beginner or anyone doubting: it only takes a little to move a mountain.

"Your faith may be just a little thread. It may be small and weak, but act on that faith. It does not matter how big your faith is, but rather, where your faith is."

Billy Graham

CHAPTER 17
The Sky's the Limit and the Story Isn't Over Yet

"Faith does not operate in the realm of the possible. There is no glory for God in that which is humanly possible. Faith begins where man's power ends."

The above quote is by George Muller (1805-1898). I read his autobiography years ago and this is what I learned. He was a devoted follower of Christ. He, in partnership with his wife, started multiple orphan homes and cared for more than ten thousand orphans during his life. He never asked anyone for a dime; he just asked God to provide. He was known as a man of prayer, and obviously, a man of great faith.

Our friend Naomi also cared for orphans during her short lifetime, through her organization Save the Widows and Orphans Foundation. Because of her faith and love for others, many orphans and widows will be taken care of for years to come, even though Naomi is gone.

Naomi was our ministry's liaison in Malawi. Her compassion for the people of the Ntecheu District, including the children that she helped care for at one of the orphan care centres my dad built, were her driving force. Throughout many years of illness, troubles and devastation, she stayed focused on her work. A widow herself and mother of one son, she sadly passed away in June of 2018.

Over the course of about five years prior to Naomi's passing, she and my dad created a strong relationship in bringing lifesaving water to villages in Ntecheu. Naomi sought out the villages that had the greatest need so Dad would know where to have the next well built.

Ever since they started working together, Dad returned home from his trips—and first things first—he'd give us an update of Naomi's condition.

Naomi had contracted the HIV virus from her husband before he died. As is customary, her husband's family came and took everything the couple had when he passed away. This young, single mom was left to raise her son on her own and battle full-blown AIDS.

Dear Reader, did you know that widows of certain cultures in many developing countries face this nightmare all the time? A woman's husband dies and she and her children are left with nothing—no money, no possessions and sometimes no home. But that's another story for a book of its own.

Praise God, a family member willed Naomi some land and that was the start of Save the Widows and Orphans Foundation. I can only imagine the praying, the hoping and the trusting involved in this seemingly impossible dream. And the people God would bring along to provide financially included Dad's Project Wellness organization. He was happy to provide fertilizer and other essentials to help get her crops started, which she shared with local orphans and widows in need.

Dad came home after a trip to report that Naomi was close

to death. After the next trip, he was thrilled to tell us she was much better. That would become normal—on death's doorstep, restored; terribly ill, feeling well. Then Naomi had another fight to face, or I should say, reason to exercise great faith; she was in a car accident. This, of course, presented a whole other gigantic hill to climb. She ultimately succumbed to tuberculosis.

This was a huge loss to her village and the orphans she helped, and of course her thirteen-year-old son, her sister and the rest of her family and friends. Dad was devastated. We all were. Chris, who got to know Naomi when he began traveling to Malawi, speaks of her incredibly bright and sunshiny smile, her love for the Lord and the less fortunate, her resilience, persistence and solid faith.

Naomi's sister took over the foundation and takes care of Naomi's son. This young man wants to be a pilot when he grows up. Having had a mother, who set such an excellent faith example, and his aunt who keeps it going, and all of us praying, nothing shall be impossible for him. Surely, the sky's the limit.

Mike and I prayed every day for a miracle of healing, and even though we believed beyond a shadow of a doubt it could happen, we put our faith in the Healer more so than the healing. As I've mentioned before, Mike's prayers were similar to Jesus' when He petitioned, "Father, if You are willing, take this cup from me; yet not my will, but Yours be done." Luke 22:42 (NIV)

Mike surrendered his own desires into the hands of God. His faith became a tower and he possessed a contentment that inspired people and magnified the Lord. Even though he longed for that miracle, he longed for Jesus more. He trusted in Him and took Him at his word, His pledge to faithfully supply, to provide rest and peace in difficult times, to never leave his side and never forsake him, and to prepare a room for him in heaven.

Chris says that when Heather was told the cancer was back and she only had a few months to live, she responded from her tower of faith with this "God has a plan for me. If it's to stay here and do His work on Earth, or if it's to be with Him in heaven, I'm ready." She went to be with Him in heaven fourteen months later.

"It's not the strength of your faith that saves you,
but the strength of Him upon whom you rely."
Charles H. Spurgeon

Chris and I have quite a long list of friends (and people we don't know) who have cancer, ALS or another illness we are praying for. We pray for healing and for miracles. But even more, we pray that each person would put their faith (if they haven't yet) in the all-powerful Saviour of the world who has already made good on God's promises.

"...God had so much loving-kindness. He loved us with such a great love. Even when we were dead because of our sins, He made us alive by what Christ did for us. You have been saved from the punishment of sin by His loving-favour. God raised us up from death when He raised up Christ Jesus. He has given us a place with Christ in the heavens...
"For by His loving-favour you have been saved from the punishment of sin through faith. It is not by anything you have done. It is a gift of God. It is not given to you because you

worked for it. If you could work for it, you would be proud. We are His work. He has made us to belong to Christ Jesus so we can work for Him. He planned that we should do this."
Ephesians 2:4-10 (NLV)

It goes without saying, but I'll say it anyway—that's GOOD NEWS!

After writing "Good News of Great Joy," I had miracles on my mind. For whatever reason, I kept thinking about Jesus' first one, where He turned water into wine. Not only did it inspire the following piece, it inspired the whole next chapter.

Fine Wine and Fireworks (and a little politics) - Jan 26, 2019

January is Mike's birthday month and the anniversary of his passing. If you are a Facebook friend, you'll know because I always post something. January 5, 2019 marked four years from when Mike left our presence— I'll never get over it. Chris and I found the only quiet place that day at the airport in Cabo San Lucas for me to let it all out. I had no idea I needed to let it all out. The tears came unannounced. We were waiting to board our flight home after spending a glorious week at the beach where Chris took me to watch the fireworks on New Year's Eve.

Chris and Heather were there four years earlier and watched the fireworks on New Year's from the resort next door from where we were. I felt so honoured to go back to that spot with Chris and take in the amazing fireworks display with him. He was remembering a beautiful moment in time that will forever bless his life. I know the feeling, and it was fun to walk down memory lane with him and to create beautiful new memories of our own. I don't think he could possibly know how much those fireworks meant to me. I was reminded of my first New Year's Eve without Mike when I stood on my balcony, recollecting our stroke-of-midnight kisses and spotting a few fireworks in the distance. I was convinced Mike set them off for me.

I can't believe it's a new year already. Each one seems to fly by a little bit faster than the last one. I never seem to accomplish everything I think I should. A couple of months ago while Erin and I were talking, I told her that I had hoped my book would be finished by now. I told her my goal was to have it written by the end of the year. She replied with something so wise. She told me that maybe all the events that are to be written about in this book haven't happened yet. She suggested the story wasn't over. I immediately became hopeful about what was still to come and stopped beating myself up for not being more disciplined.

Sure enough, some things have happened that add to the story. Like this thing. In early December, Chris and I got a call from Dan Ruimy (our MP), inviting us to come to Ottawa where a group of MPs were hosting a reception for people of the Christian faith. They called it "Christmas on the Hill." He explained that on the Hill, they honour different days and events celebrated by people of different faiths, so they agreed it would be nice to do the same for some of their Christian constituents. Dan said that after hearing our story from Chris, he was so impressed by our faith that he thought of us when this Christmas on the Hill event came up.

Chris told Dan our story on their recent trip to Malawi. Dan and his assistant, Khalida, joined Dad and Chris in November to see firsthand three more wells drilled. Khalida sponsored one in honour of her dad and mom.

Dan and Khalida and Dad have been friends since Dad went into their office to check Dan out and to introduce himself shortly after Dan was elected. Khalida and Dan have been extremely kind to Dad and to our family. They tirelessly and joyfully serve the communities of Pitt Meadows and Maple Ridge.

Of course, Elanna and Dad were invited to Ottawa as well. Peter could have come, but someone had to stay home and work, plus I think the air mile points had surely run out.

It was an honour to meet our Prime Minister, Justin Trudeau, and present him with a copy of my book. Dad shook his hand first and told him that as a Christian missionary, he prays for him every day. You could tell the Prime Minister was touched and very grateful. Dad made sure I was next. I definitely wasn't as articulate as I said a few words. The Prime Minister graciously accepted my book, and then I introduced him to Elanna and Chris. While Chris and he compared socks (Chris knows he's a sock guy and asked to see them), I realized I didn't get the picture I wanted. I quickly elbowed my way through the crowd to notify Justin's assistant, who was now holding my book. She was way too busy for my problem, as she was trying to keep the Prime Minister on time and slowly ushered him toward the exit. I stayed close to the crowd as everyone took their turn meeting him and getting their picture taken. I didn't want to be greedy, but I just had to get that photo; I stayed hopeful.

Sure enough, as his assistant gave him the final head-nod—we're done here— he looked right at me, stepped forward, and reached for my hand. I apologized for taking more of his time and explained the situation. In one motion, he took my book, put his arm around me and smiled handsomely for the camera.

It was a thrilling three-day adventure. Dan and Khalida took us on a couple of tours of the Parliament buildings, including the House of Commons. We met a number of other MPs and Ministers. We also sat in on a question period where Dan honoured Dad in the House again. Some of his speech went like this: "Mr. Speaker, you may remember a year ago, I rose to celebrate my constituent George Klassen's 80th birthday and the work he does drilling wells with Project Wellness. Well, Mr. Speaker, I took a week of personal time to join George and what an incredible journey it was. I saw firsthand the impact fresh water brings to a village. They can grow crops and they no longer have to drink from the river they bathe in. This leads to less sickness and disease which leads to better health."

Composed Dan showed a little emotion at the end when he concluded, "Mr. Speaker, this Christmas will be the most special to me." It was so well said, and Dad received a standing ovation. By the way, both videos can be viewed on our website projectwellness.ca.

I'm not really into politics. I always had to ask Mike (who was very much into politics) who's who and what's what. Now, Chris (also knowledgeable in politics) gets to answer all my questions. I rarely participate in political debates, especially on social media, and I try to take my judgments to the Lord. I pray about certain issues that I really care about, of course, but since our trip to Ottawa, I'm taking my duty as a Christian to pray for our politicians and leaders more seriously and to fervently pray for our nation. May hearts be turned to God and His will be done!

I thought it was pretty cool that the following verses showed up in our daily reading the first few days back from Ottawa:

"You are the light of the world. A city set on a hill cannot be hidden. Nor do people light a lamp and put it under a basket, but on a stand, and it gives light to all in the house. In the same way, let your light shine before others, so that they may see your good works and give glory to your Father who is in heaven."
Matthew 5:14-16 (ESV)

December was a whirlwind with a couple of trips, Christmas, and the death of our dear friend, Chuck. Chuck's passing happened first actually, on December 2nd. In my last blog post, "Good News of Great Joy,"

I wrote about my remarkable warrior friend Shonia, who has persevered beyond what most people could in a heroic battle with cancer. I also mentioned another friend in hospice. That was Chuck. Chuck is the friend I reconnected with at Elanna's workplace (from Chapter 13).

Chuck was diagnosed with MS in 1975; he had to give up working in 1986 and quietly and patiently endured increasing pain and suffering all these years. One thing mentioned a number of times at his memorial service last weekend was his positive attitude and his incredible perseverance. This wonderful, gentle man described by family and friends was exactly the man I knew. He always wanted to know about you, and he had the most beautiful smile.

While I was visiting Chuck a couple of weeks before he died, I tried with all my might to make him smile. It was always really easy to get a smile from Chuck. But on this day, there seemed to be no way until I mentioned our first meeting in heaven. When I said how I looked forward to seeing him in heaven and hearing all the things he'd been trying to say, a smile came. When I reminded him of the new legs he was getting and no need for wheelchairs there, his smile increased. I assured him that the best was yet to come! His wife, Beth, said that's how she had been speaking to him. Elanna said the same thing.

I'm sure "the best is yet to come" conversations brought joy and hope to Chuck's weary bones and that the Bible verses Beth read to him in his final days brought reassurance and peace. By the grace of God, now he's free—the best has come for Chuck!

I started a new blog post a couple of weeks ago. My idea was to take off from where I left off in my last one. I had miracles on my mind, in particular Jesus' first – where He turns water into wine. Once I got started researching this story, I couldn't stop. The topic led to writing a whole chapter for my book. Compared to the other miracles, I thought this one was just ho-hum … but it's the complete opposite!

In my water-to-wine chapter, I listed some quotes and notes regarding different views and opinions. I focused on two that really speak to me and are very unique. I'll keep those between me and Chapter Eighteen for now, and share these two ideas that work well with this piece:

* "The best is yet to come" OR "The best for last." The idea is that the closer we get to Him, the better it gets until we are in His presence, and then the best has come. Until then, as we continue to seek Him, we are changed from glory to glory.

* This first sign is a demonstration that He is the source of all true and lasting joy. Don't settle for the cheap stuff. Replace the cheap wine with the best imaginable.

I'm not a wine drinker and have no idea what to look for in a good bottle of wine. The few times I've bought wine to take to a host or if someone was coming over, I shopped for it by the label. If the label was aesthetically pleasing—certain colours and design—sold!

Anyway, I share the first idea in light of Chuck's passing, and since then my uncle John's passing (Dad's brother), who endured Parkinson's Disease for many years. I share the second idea because it fits with a sermon I just heard.

Once in a while I go to a church called God Rock in Port Coquitlam on Saturday nights, where Nathan drums sometimes. I wrote about a really cool experience I had in this church last year, where I had a vision of Mike leaving his body when he died. It's from my post "From Here to There in Three Years."

God Rock isn't the kind of church most people imagine when they hear the word "church." This is a church where a lot of people in recovery meet (recovering addicts). It's not a church for someone who has a problem with a bunch of smokers lighting up outside the front doors. People don't get all dressed up here. They come as they are and let me tell you, God is there!

The sermon was convicting and filled with the grace, love and the power of the Holy Spirit, like the other ones I've heard. This young, buff, on-fire-for-Jesus preacher named BJ gave a message called "Gospel 101—How to Become a Christian" (and how to share your faith with others). He started, "We are going to talk about how to be set apart to the glory of Jesus Christ. I have four points. Number one…" Right away, I thought about the little booklet my dad uses to share his faith and how he has taught countless others how to do the same.

BJ's points: 1. God is great. 2. We reject God. 3. God gives grace. 4. We give God all of our life. Dad's booklet points (just from memory, so not exact): 1. God loves us and has the best plans for our lives. 2. Sin separates us from knowing God. 3. Through Jesus we can know God personally. 4. We must accept and receive Jesus as Lord and Savior to be forgiven of our sins and know God personally. Dad's booklet has a little picture of a throne and asks the reader, "Where are you and where is God in relation to the throne of your life? (Booklet title: *Have You Heard of the Four Spiritual Laws?* by Bill Bright)

BJ's and Dad's points are worded differently, but it's the same message; they both urge the reader/listener to give their life to Christ. BJ had his own "throne" illustration at the end. He told us that "believing" isn't enough. The Bible says that even the demons believe (James 2:19). In order to receive Jesus and become a Christian, you must give all of your life to Him. You relinquish your old sinful life for a new life. He explained it as an exchange. Enthusiastically, he proclaimed, "All of Him for all of me? Yes please!"

He told the congregation it can be a struggle, of course. It's hard for everyone to leave everything with Him, and then not try to take some things back again. I'm pretty sure that Chuck and my uncle John, who both recently entered into the presence of God, would testify that it's a glorious exchange. Cheering us on to give it all up for Him!

Dad's booklet includes a suggested prayer. It goes something like this: "Jesus, I need You. Thank you for dying on the cross for my sins. Please forgive me and come into my life. I receive you as my Lord and Saviour. Help me to trust in You. Amen"

As much as I thought a couple of months ago that my book would never be written, I now feel like I'm getting close. The story isn't over though, of course.

Hey, if you have breath, your story isn't over yet; God has great plans for your life! So, what do you say? If you're still settling for that cheap wine, why not replace it with the very best: Jesus!

Praise God for His blood which washes away every stain!

Happy New Year, friends! And Dear Chris, thanks for the fireworks!

He turned water into wine, gave sight to the blind, restored the paralyzed. He breathes fresh breath into the lifeless; His power is timeless. There is nobody like Him.

CHAPTER 18

The Best is Yet to Come, and What Grief and Cherry Blossoms have in Common

"With His own will He can do all things for us and in a moment turn the waters of our grief into joy."

Charles H. Spurgeon

When Chris and I were planning our wedding, I asked our friend, the officiant to-be, Pastor Glen, if he could perhaps speak on something other than love. I know that sounds odd. In particular, I suggested he not speak from the popular 1 Corinthians 13 verses: "Love is patient, love is kind…" It's weirdly specific, and to me, now, sounds ridiculous. Plus, Glen hadn't given us any indication that he planned to use the famous verses or any other traditional wedding script. He was kind to ask if we had any thoughts on topics though, and I jumped in with a few.

The typical love stuff is very appropriate for the wedding of a young couple starting out, but Chris and I already had a lot of years of marriage under our belts. Not that we had perfected the art of loving a spouse, but we had had a lot of practice being "patient and kind." I thought another message might be nice … you know, refreshing … like Jesus turning water into wine. I've recently learned that the water-to-wine story is an excellent lesson in love after all.

One of my suggestions was a story in the book of John about the wedding at Cana where Jesus performs His first miracle (the first miracle recorded in the Bible). John calls it a "sign." I don't know why I suggested it, except that it's a story that takes place at a wedding and there's this first miracle, which I didn't even think was really that special. Jesus turns water into wine. I don't like wine at all, and this miracle, in my opinion, paled in comparison to other miracles. It didn't save anyone's life or even change anyone's life like the others do. Or so I thought, until I took a better look.

There are other "bigger" miracles to read about. I've even written about Jesus walking on water and calming storms. In one of my favourite stories, Jesus heals a woman who had been bleeding for twelve years. This Jewess, ostracized and held captive by the religious laws pertaining to menstruation at the time, risked it all when she made her way through the crowd surrounding Jesus and touched the fringe of his garment. At the end of her rope, surely she hoped to just get close enough to touch His clothes … or to simply breathe the same air He did.

I learned a lot about it many moons ago when I wrote my blog post "Take Hold of His Robe." I love the part where Jesus questions the group, asking, "Who touched me?" The woman only touched the edge of His robe, but He knew. When she confessed it was her, He called her "daughter" and said her faith made her well. He took no credit; He credited her faith. Wow! This story remains one of my favourites since Max Lucado made it come to life for me in his book *He Still Moves Stones*, which I first read many years ago and since then, have read a few more times.

Perhaps the most well-known miracle is when Jesus fed five thousand (plus) people with just five loaves of bread and two fish. Also called "Bread of Life," Jesus provides a feast for the multitudes, satisfying their hunger in more ways than one. Can you believe there were leftovers? I love leftovers. I wonder if the disciples had a cool place to store the extras and then got excited the next day when they remembered them, like I do. This story has encouraged my faith many times, and I've often prayed "Fishes and loaves, Lord. Fishes and loaves" when I or someone I know has needed something to go further than seemed possible.

During His three-year ministry preceding His ultimate mission—His reason for leaving His home in heaven and becoming a baby, a boy, a man and a sacrifice—Jesus miraculously healed the sick, the blind, the deaf, the mute, the paralyzed. He healed the demon-possessed and even raised people from the dead! So this first miracle of turning water into wine seems unnecessary, even silly, like a waste of everyone's time. Until you dig deeper.

Jewish wedding celebrations could last up to a week. I've read that even though drunkenness was improper in the Jewish culture, so was a lack of wine. Running out of wine was actually a crime. It was a major social embarrassment to the point of shame and disgrace and even legal ramifications.

The party had already been going strong for days when Mary told Jesus the wine had run dry. He questioned why she involved Him and told her His time had not yet come. Note that in other Scriptures, this referred to His time of death and resurrection. But in this case, maybe He was referring to His time to perform signs that reveal who He really is—the Messiah, God's Son. Seemingly not understanding or not listening or just being extremely hopeful, Mary proceeded to tell the servers to do exactly what Jesus asked them to do, almost knowing He was going to come to the rescue. It's not said whose wedding it was but some references I've read suggest it was a family member or close friend, which explains Mary's concern.

Chris and I recently spent seven glorious days at an all-inclusive in Cabo San Lucas, Mexico. Beautiful smiling faces welcomed us with an "Hola" and a glass of champagne. Chris and I don't drink (I've never been a drinker and Chris quit drinking cold-turkey four years ago), but I made an exception and drank about half. The expectation was "all you could eat" and "all you could drink" from time of arrival to departure. Had the resort ran out of booze, we wouldn't have minded at all, but there would have been many very disgruntled vacationers.

I'm guessing that's what weddings were like when Mary urged her son to do something in this uncomfortable situation. Jesus seemed to hesitate, but then told the servers to fill six stone water jars with water. Each jar (used for ceremonial washing) held twenty to thirty gallons and were filled to the brim. Jesus then told the servers to take some to the master of ceremonies. After having a drink, the master of ceremonies, knowing nothing about Jesus' transformation of water to wine, pulled the groom aside and commended him for saving the best wine for last. Unlike what is customary, the best was served first.

This miracle wasn't meant to wow a crowd with the glory

of God, but instead was a private display for a select few: the servers, Jesus' disciples and dear old Mom. I don't know about Mary, but if my son had just performed his first miracle, I'd be posting that news to Facebook with pictures and maybe video. That's what's customary for me when my children do impressive things.

Mary already knew who her son was; she got the memo before He was born. But perhaps the disciples needed a sign to chase away any doubts and take their commitment to Jesus to the next level. John 2:11 says, "This act in Cana of Galilee was the first sign Jesus gave, the first glimpse of his glory. And his disciples believed in Him." (Message)

Later it says in John 20:30-31 (NIV), "Jesus performed many other signs in the presence of His disciples, which are not recorded in this book. But these are written that you may believe that Jesus is the Messiah, the Son of God, and that by believing you may have life in His name."

I have spent a considerable amount of time now studying this water-to-wine sign. One article leads to another, to a video, to a sermon, to a podcast, and so on. This piece started out as my next blog post, but when I realized it was bigger than that, I happily decided to make it a chapter in this book. I just really enjoyed the investigating.

The more I studied this miracle, the further in love I fell with Jesus. And I thought to myself, *Maybe the readers will fall deeper in love with Him as well. Maybe doubters will believe; maybe skeptics will receive. Perhaps it will change a life or two ... or five thousand.*

When I began my research, I started by Googling a couple of preacher/teachers I used to listen to on the radio all the time: Greg Laurie and Chuck Swindoll. I started tuning in when I taught the group fitness instructor course at Douglas College in New Westminster. That was such a great job! My friend Grace trained me and gave me that job. I taught other people to do what I loved—instruct exercise classes. I taught the twenty-eight-hour course, which ran evenings and Saturdays for roughly ten years, from about 1997 to 2007.

Anyway, on the forty-five-or-so minute drive home at night, I listened to Greg Laurie preach, followed by Chuck Swindoll. My mom and dad listened to them first. Mom often told me how great they were and how I should tune in. I did, and I got hooked.

In one of Greg Laurie's teachings on the water-to-wine story, he focused on this concept: the best is yet to come because Jesus saves His best wine for last. The message was about inviting Jesus into every aspect of your life, for example your marriage, and it would be blessed. Not perfect but blessed. He said that as believers, every day we become a little more like Him as He transforms us. He said that even though we age, and our bodies deteriorate, a new body awaits us and a heaven that will "surpass our wildest dreams." For those who have put their faith in Christ, the best is yet to come.

In another water-to-wine message, he and others I've read, including Chuck Swindoll, talked about the unlimited power of God. How Jesus can make the impossible possible.

There are so many takeaways from this story. In one after another, they brought God more and more glory and caused my heart to soar. Here are a few of my favourite findings (some notes and quotes). The first two ideas I shared in the last chapter:

* The best is yet to come, or best for last. As you continue to follow Jesus and obey Him, you will be supernaturally changed from glory to glory, until we are in His presence: "And we all, with unveiled face, beholding the glory of the Lord, are being transformed into the same image from one degree of glory to another. For this comes from the Lord who is the Spirit." 2 Corinthians 3:18 (ESV)

* In the Jewish culture, wine symbolized joy. Some explain that the first miracle is about perpetual joy and that Jesus is the source of all true and lasting joy. Don't settle for cheap wine. Jesus provides the greatest, lasting joy and anything else you put in that place will eventually let you down. And there is this: Jesus is referred to as the Bridegroom in Scripture; the church is His bride (the church, meaning all believers). He is the provider ... of food, drink, ultimate joy.

* "The couple ran out of wine. What have you run out of?" Tom Haugen. Ask Jesus for help. When you ask for help, it's like saying, "I can't Lord, but You can." When we ask and obey, life transformation happens.

* Jesus cares about the details of our lives—the little things, big things and everything in between. May we not miss His acts of love and kindness.

* "It is good to run short, so that we may be driven to the Lord by our necessity, for He will more than supply it." Charles. H. Spurgeon

* When Jesus saves the party by turning water into wine, He is basically saying that He is the true Master of ceremonies.

Many viewpoints focus on asking, on obeying, on believing, on trusting, on expecting, and on experiencing true joy. Many speak of the transforming power of Jesus, His kindness and compassion; how He cares about the details of our lives and how He provides. Here are two final impactful points I'd like to share:

* Pastor Mark Evans from Believers Church says in his YouTube video sermon, "The whole thing God needs us to know is that when He touches the natural, it becomes supernatural." He says we all have the natural thing, meaning life and breath, but when that natural pot has been anointed by the touch of God, everything in it becomes supernatural.

* A young man by the name of Jon Jorgensen said in his YouTube three-part mini-sermon series about this beloved water-to-wine sign, that Jesus was pointing to the Gospel— to His death and resurrection. He explained that Jesus was making a case for who He was and is, the Saviour of the world, and noted that at some point, we become empty. He says that Mary is a good example—she turns to Jesus when the wine runs out. Wine represents the blood of Jesus. Empty people were completely transformed when Jesus came and poured out new good wine—His blood on the cross for the sins of the world.

If we just skimmed the surface of this story, we might think it's about keeping the party alive and the buzz going. But the Bible actually warns not to get drunk on wine, but instead be filled with the Spirit (Ephesians 5:18). That, together with my above findings, tells us this isn't at all about the temporary high and the quick and fleeting fix of excessive wine, but instead the complete opposite. It's about the permanent, transforming, healing and redeeming power of God.

While on our recent trip to Cabo, Chris took me to the

resort next door to ours, where he and Heather had their last vacation together four years before. He showed me around and pointed out where they sat by the pool, where they ate meals, where they walked on the beach, and where they watched fireworks on New Year's Eve. He also showed me where he had his last drink. He said he was relying on the alcohol to get him through, drowning his sorrows and numbing the pain.

But to be the best caregiver for Heather, he knew what he had to do. By the transforming power of God, he stopped drinking that last day of their holiday. It wasn't easy, of course, and Chris says it sometimes still isn't. Chris confessed when our trip was over that he struggled a little bit for the first couple of days. He can't do it in his own strength but relies on the Lord every step of the way.

So, when you go below the surface and get into the depths of this water-to-wine story, you find this marvellous treasure chest of God's exceeding glory. It's definitely about a miracle that changes and saves lives. Jesus satisfies thirst and hunger; He turns doubt to belief, trouble to relief, despair and grief to joy and peace. And even more than all that, He turned His body (broken bread) and His blood (poured-out wine) into eternal hope and everlasting life. It's summed up in one word: LOVE! He is summed up in one word: LOVE!

Back when I suggested this scripture from John Chapter 2 to Pastor Glen for our wedding, I just thought it was cool—this first miracle of Jesus' at Cana of Galilee. Now, it means so much more to me and I relate to its truths in my life: the natural becomes supernatural at His command; the ordinary becomes extraordinary!

Before I started writing on a regular basis, but dreamt of

being a writer someday, I thought of this title for my imaginary book: An Ordinary Life in the Hands of an Extraordinary God. Maybe it was somewhat prophetic. Although it's not the title of my first book or this one, it is what I write about. The supernatural and the extraordinary don't just happen though. They come when we submit and commit our lives to Him. The very best is always in His mind for us, but there is a role we play—surrender, follow Him and obey. I should add, that doesn't mean we get what we want and everything is rosy. It means we get what He wants, what He knows is best for us in the long run.

It's like the servers in our story. They had to do what Jesus told them to do to experience the supernatural, to be a part of the extraordinary. It wouldn't have been easy. Those pots were huge, and, of course, there was no running water.

I occasionally dig in my heels when the Lord tells me to do something. I look at those huge pots and think it's too much, or I simply pretend I don't hear Him. But when I follow through, it's like, why did I disobey Him the last time? It's never worth it. I've never regretted filling the pots.

"If you know that God loves you, you should never question a directive from Him."
Henry Blackaby

Today is Mike's birthday, I am writing this paragraph (and I wrote the last two) from his favourite table at Wendel's Cafe in Fort Langley. I came alone to get some writing done and to spend some time with my thoughts and memories of him. I am a little emotional, but also feel courageous and inspired by my own water-to-wine experiences. So, I thought I'd share something I have never said out loud before. Here goes, I married Chris out of obedience. I know it doesn't sound very romantic when I put it that way, but it felt like a calling almost. Let me explain why I refer to it as a step of obedience: Even though I fell deeply in love with Chris very quickly, there were obstacles in the way.

Here are two of a few: 1. Fear. I was terrified of the inevitable goodbye I'd have to say someday to another love of my life. 2. I was feeling conflicted. Even though my children were adults, I didn't want to disregard how they felt. We had been through a lot together and there were so many changes, and again, this change happened so fast. One day, feeling torn, I called out to God and said, "What about my kids?" The response was immediate. "I've got your kids—they are going to be just fine. Trust me, I have the best plans for all of you in mind and My timing is always right."

When Chris and I got married, the obstacles didn't just disappear. Honestly, I think new ones appeared. It hasn't been perfectly smooth sailing. A couple of bumps have caused me to question, *Did I hear correctly? Did we go too quickly?* I'm sure Chris has quietly asked the same thing. Nevertheless, I can't imagine my life without him. And most of the 620 days we've been husband and wife, I've been floating around on cloud nine. On those uncertain days, I've been comforted when God reminded me that I obeyed Him. I filled the water pots to the brim. I entrusted my ordinary life into the hands of an extraordinary God, and the wine is perfecting. I should say, the wine is perfection. And I can't imagine my life without Him!

Sometimes I wonder if Mike had a role in choosing

Chris for me. That might sound a little crazy, but he could have prayed about it, in which case he did have a say in it. Perhaps he had a mental list: similarities between him and the man he was praying about on one side, and differences on the other. He may have prayed, "Dear Lord, please give her someone who excels in patience and kindness. And of course, someone who's going to make her laugh a lot. Give her someone who goes above and beyond when it comes to caring, giving and showing love. Can you bless her with someone who will treat her like the beautiful and amazing gift she is? Give her a man who will pour himself out for her and our kids. And in contrast to me, can you give her someone who is handy with tools, good with the books, and techie?" If his prayers went anything like that, they were answered.

It was almost as if Mike was with me and Chris on our first date (second date, I guess, if you count when we first met for coffee). Chris said the same Jack Nicholson quote that Mike always had when we went out to eat. It was from the movie, Five Easy Pieces during the restaurant scene where a difficult waitress wouldn't accommodate Jack's special order. So Jack ordered off the menu and proceeded to tell her to hold this and hold that, and then eventually said, "And I want you to hold it between your knees."

Mike quoted this line to almost every waitress we ever had (and I would give the confused server the look like, *Don't mind him, he's a little cuckoo*). So when Chris said it on that first date (with the perfect Jack Nicolson voice, I might add), I was shocked. I couldn't believe it. It was like a set up. Mike would have laughed hysterically. While holding his belly and gasping for breath, he would probably have said, "Okay, you pass!" My thought was, *And so the joy continues.*

A recent prayer of mine: *Dear Heavenly Father, please give this message to Mike: Hi Mike! You are dearly and often painfully missed by so many of us - me and the kids, family and friends. I want you to know that while I'm still so sad that you are gone, I'm okay. I'm actually really great. Joy and grief continue to coexist in my life quite nicely. I've gotten used to it. Thanks again for the abundant joy you brought me and the laughter and exceeding love. You helped me really appreciate and cherish those priceless gifts. And the joy, laughter and love continue! I will see you when I see you, and until then, you are forever in my heart, often on my mind and I still talk about you all the time. P.S. The kids are great and you'd be more proud of them than ever. They are incredible human beings. I continue to see so much of you in each of them and it blesses me beyond measure.*

And Father, this one's for Heather: *Hi Heather, I just want to say that your incredible love and devotion helped shape Chris into the outstanding man and wonderful husband he is today. Thank you! With God's help, I'll continue to love him the way he deserves ... and more, if that's possible. Even though we've never met, I feel like I know you well through stories and pictures and, most of all, your beautiful girls. In them I see your compassion, generosity, strength and courage; I see your gorgeous smile and kind, loving heart. I just want you to know that I'm here for them and I'll do my best to support and encourage them for as long as I can. I pray for them, along with my own children, every day.*

And Jesus continues to beckon, "Obey, believe, trust Me and enjoy My love.

Enjoy, My love!

And don't forget: the best is yet to come!"

What Grief and Cherry Blossoms Have in Common
- April 8, 2019

Spring has sprung and I feel like a new person. Even though I adore the fall and am quick to proclaim it's my favourite season of all, spring rejuvenates my soul. I'm pretty sure a lot of us feel that way. After a few months of rationed sunlight, cold temperatures, grey skies and rain, it's like we come to life again when spring shows its pretty face. It's been raining on and off today, but here in Metro Vancouver, we've had some lovely weather lately. I'm a bit of a light junkie. The longer days, blue skies and sun shining right in my eyes makes my heart sing.

Every spring I rethink my "favourite" season and am never sad to say goodbye to winter. In fact, "Good riddance!" Our winters are rarely the gently-falling-snowflakes and bright-skies kind. They are mostly the damp, darkish, often rainy, sometimes slushy kind. Grief is like our winter. But like grief and every Vancouver winter, sooner or later you see the light of day at the end of the grey tunnel.

Spring break recently came and went. I scurried home the last day of school with my list of things to do, in no particular order: finish writing my book, go to my friend Donna's wedding, babysit Leah and Glen the grand-dog, hang out with family and friends, get together with brother-in-law Gary (who was in town on business), and go away for a few days with Chris. Halfway through the two weeks of bliss and my amazing list, I was caught off-guard by some major grief. I kept thinking, *This isn't supposed to be happening; it's spring.* But like

I learned long ago, grief can come from out of nowhere. It's impartial to the day of the week and season.

This interruption was a reminder that at any given time, I could easily be just one sad story away from the ugliest crying you've ever seen (some might call it a full-on breakdown; others might say it could have something to do with perimenopause). The sermon at church included a few sad stories and that's what did it for me.

Chris and I had been at our friends' wedding just the day before, and those tears had joy written all over them. I was so happy for these two—my friend Donna who was married for forty-three years to her high school sweetheart Neil, who passed away from ALS (whom I told you about earlier), and Jory (whom Chris and I were so blessed to meet just a few weeks before), who was married for thirty-eight years to Robin, who passed away due to Alzheimer's disease.

It was the most beautiful outdoor service in False Creek, and during the equally beautiful indoor reception I caught a glimpse of the memorial table for the bride's and groom's late spouses. The picture of Neil, my friend who was like a brother, grabbed my attention and melted my heart, and reminded me of how much I missed him. I thought a lot about the two families coming together—the two daughters of Donna and the two daughters of Jory, in particular. I could only imagine how bittersweet the occasion might have been for them. They honoured their mom and dad (and new stepdad and stepmom) so wonderfully. You could already see how blessed they all are going to be to share their journeys of grief and love with each other.

Jory's brother, the pastor who officiated the service, gave a short but powerful message. He said something along these lines—"It takes an incredible love and a lot of courage for these two, having gone through what they have, to enter into another marriage." I appreciated how he drew attention to the courage!

Anyway, the next day after church when Chris and I were getting ready to go away, I lost it (I'm talking really lost it). I felt the tears just below the surface earlier, as I was already feeling something stirring when Pastor Ezra shared a few troubling stories about people he knew in his home country of Kenya. That's when the tears surfaced. At the end, he shared his own sad story; the grief and the pastor's vulnerability were overwhelming for me. A couple of hours later, the tears were streaming. Chris and I had to postpone our getaway.

The next day when I tried to explain, I told Chris it was a variety of things. I told him that the sermon was the straw that broke the camel's back. There are so many sad things happening in this world near and far, and some of those things had been weighing on my heart. Of course, missing people is always a catalyst to deeper sadness, in this case, Neil, my mom—and always Mike. I also explained I was a little anxious about leaving certain people, including a certain dog, even for a few days, which seemed crazy.

Chris and I did manage to get away. They were

pretty quiet days; peaceful and low-key. AND, drum roll please, I finished my book while we were gone! I'll be going over it a few more times though, fine tuning until it's truly done and I'm ready to let it go.

My cousin Julie recently said something that has stuck with me (not that I didn't know this about myself already). Casually in conversation, she mentioned how I like to keep my cards close, which comes from the saying "Keep your cards close to your chest," like in a card game so people can't see them. Julie is perceptive and smart and can read people well, but mostly she just knows me and how I roll. Everyone has a story and I love hearing them. I really admire and appreciate vulnerability, authenticity and when a person shows who they are and shares it from the heart without fear of being judged. I have a tendency to hold back. So as I go over my book from beginning to end again and again, I'm constantly asking God and myself, *Am I being vulnerable enough? Am I being a window? Am I fully trusting Him?*

Moving on to the next Sunday, I got up and started getting ready for church. Chris asked if I'd like to go downtown to see the cherry blossom trees instead. As much as I was looking forward to Ezra's next sermon on the Book of Ruth part two, I replied with a definite "Yes!" Chris mentioned it was the only time we could see these particular cherry blossom trees before he left on his upcoming trip to Malawi. I later saw he had a list of all the best cherry blossom trees in the Lower Mainland—where they are, when they bloom, etc. I was so touched. His thoughtfulness never ceases to amaze me.

Earlier, I said that grief was like winter. Here's why. Winter might not be as lovely as spring, summer or fall, but it's not a complete write-off when it comes to beauty. You might just have to look harder. It's not colourful or fragrant or warm, but there are certain aspects of it that are exceedingly lovely—and that's like grief. Grief has a way of drawing us nearer to the Lord. When we draw near to God, He draws near to us (James 4:8). In this closeness, we experience the depths of His mercy, His exemplary love and His healing touch.

So, what grief and cherry blossom trees have in common is that they both draw us closer to God. Sorrowful things and beautiful things have a way of revealing His tender heart. Even though it is spring and cherry blossom season, it might also be a season of grieving for you. If so, I hope you can embrace both. And I hope you know that God is with you wherever you are and wherever you go - including deep valleys of despair - He will surely be your Refuge there.

Chris and Dad are in Malawi again, drilling another three wells, including my Uncle John's memorial well. Chris has now gone to Malawi five times—that's one more time than I've been. How amazing! I am so proud of him and, of course, my dad, who at eighty-one keeps serving the Lord by taking care of widows and orphans.

Dad at Uncle John's memorial well in Malawi.

It was Leah's tenth birthday yesterday and it's Luke's eighteenth birthday tomorrow. Happy birthday to these two outstanding young people I'm so blessed to know and get to watch grow. The following verse is for them and all our children, grandchildren, nieces and nephews, young people and older, and everyone (I added the words in bold):

"Nothing can ever separate us from God's love. Neither death nor life, neither angels nor demons, neither our fears for today nor our worries about tomorrow—not even the powers of hell can separate us from the **vast, massive, incomparable, unconditional, high and wide, King-sized**, love of God!"

Romans 8:28

The more I learn about God's high and wide, King-sized love, the less I can fathom the expanse of it. The margins just keep getting moved out farther and farther. All glory, praise and honour be to Him! Amen!

I'm just wrapping up the writing of this book today on April 19, which is Good Friday. This morning, Chris brought one of his devotional books to me in bed. Most days we read and pray in the morning, so I didn't think much of it, except I usually select a book from my bedside table, or he pulls something up on the internet. I asked him if he wanted me to read.

"Sure," he responded enthusiastically.

I opened it to today's date and read the first sentence in my head. I was immediately reminded of the lump in my throat and the knot in my stomach the first time I heard it. I smiled and got choked up a little and then was like, "Wow, how do you remember dates like that?"

Three years ago, on April 19 (which would have been about six weeks after we met—when I received Chris' letter), we were reading and praying over the phone together. Chris read the first few words from the daily reader titled, *Jesus Calling* by Sarah Young, and then stopped. The writing is from the perspective of Jesus; He's doing the talking.

"Here is what it says," stated Chris. "I love you..." He paused for what seemed way longer than the few seconds it was, and continued, "...regardless of how well you are performing."

Chris had no idea the reading that day was going to start this way. He proceeded to read to the end. When he had finished (and my heart rate had returned to normal again), he continued, "Nadine?"

I reluctantly replied, "Yes, Chris?"

"I love you," he said.

You may have guessed it, another long pause followed. Later, I told him the feeling was mutual, but I couldn't say the words yet. I had never told another man, other than Mike, that I loved him. I was going to need some time to wrap my mind around that one.

On April 19, in this little devotional book, Jesus professes His unfailing, unconditional love to the reader, a love without "limits" or "conditions." He reminds us that there is nothing we can do to lose, gain or change the love He has for us.

He loves me and He loves you. Is the feeling mutual?

Once you realize He has always loved you—before you were born, before you ever heard of Him, while you still rejected and maybe even mocked Him—once you swing wide open the door of your life and invite Him and His redeeming love to come inside, to deliver hope, to make you whole ... well, you can't help but love Him back with all your heart and soul.

Acknowledgements

Thank you to everyone who helped and/or inspired me to make this book a reality, including the following:

My mom and dad who have always been my biggest cheerleaders. They told complete strangers about my first book. They handed out many copies (Dad still does) to friends, family and people they didn't know; strangers in airports, in lineups, in restaurants and so on. Mom called it my "love story." She would be so excited and so proud to share this book with the world as well … a continued love story. Thank you both for your steadfast love, devoted prayers and wonderful praise.

Elanna, my big sister and best friend who has been there for me through thick and thin. You've been a pillar, a lifter, a help in times of trouble. Thanks for cheering me on and for all the prayers, laughs and love. And to Peter, Michaela and Luke, thank you as well for your continued love and support. You four are such a wonderful family and you make a great team!

Erin, Nathan and Madison, I marvel at the wonderful qualities you inherited from your dad. Of the many, your determination and courage has inspired me in my writing and other areas of my life. I'm so thankful for each of you, for the joy you bring me, for the laughs and love and for your support and encouragement.

Leah, you are like sunshine on a gloomy day. You enrich my life in so many ways. Emerson, your kindness at such a young age warms my heart. You both bring so much joy to my life and make this world a better place. Katrina, Nathan and Lucas, great job parenting these two!

Alexa, Nicola and Frank, thank you for welcoming me into your family so readily and for allowing me to be a part of your world. It's been such a blessing and joy so far. Thanks for your kindness, encouragement and love.

Chris, where do I start? You're an amazing partner, husband, friend and personal assistant! Your patience, support, help, advice, encouragement, humour, praise and prayers during this project and since our first days together have been a huge blessing—a brilliant gift from the Lord! Thanks for pouring out your love, and for your listening ears, broad shoulders and tight hugs. I'm so grateful to God that He led you to my first book and that you had the courage and vulnerability to reach out to me.

Thank you to my pre-proofreaders, Karen, Donna, Jory and Auntie Vicki. Thank you also for cheering me on and for your feedback and encouragement.

Jory, thank you for the amazing Foreword. I am humbled and blessed by your words. You have a wonderful way with words.

Melanie Saxton, your editing skills are top notch and same with your gift of encouragement. Thanks for your praise and for stretching me.

Janine Boudreau, thank you for the beautiful book cover and for being so patient with me.

Thank you Jeannine Lode for hand lettering my title. I love it.

Michaela, thanks for helping me with my book cover and other ideas. You are an incredible artist and you're only getting started. I'm excited to see what your future holds. Elanna, thank you for your input about the cover as well. The yellow bird was a great idea.

Julie and Greg from Influence Publishing, thank you for your expert guidance and advice. And to the many authors of Influence, you inspire me.

Thank you Dana, Karen, Tom and Andy for your testimonials. Your excellent reviews mean so much to me. I'm honoured and blessed.

To everyone who is a part of this story; everyone I've written about or mentioned in this book or in my blog; it's an honour. Thank you!

Thank you to my blog readers, you've helped me persevere in my writing. You've been kind and encouraging.

To everyone effected by ALS; those living with the illness and those who are gone, including my beloved Michael and other friends, thank you for teaching the rest of us very valuable lessons in hope, courage, perseverance and love. To the caregivers and family members, you are in my prayers.

To my Heavenly Father, thank You for helping me with every word. Thank You for Your amazing grace and extravagant love that inspired me to write this book. You are merciful, faithful and so good. All glory be to You God!

Author Biography

Nadine Sands was married to Michael Sands for twenty-six years when Mike passed away due to the effects of ALS. They raised their three children in Nadine's hometown of Maple Ridge and were blessed with one granddaughter, who was five years old when Mike died.

Nadine describes writing as a calling. Shortly after Mike's diagnosis, she started her blog, "ALS With Courage." It was a great way to reveal Mike's incredible spirit and it was like therapy for her. Never in Nadine's wildest dreams did she think it would inspire a following, but soon she was connecting with fellow caregivers and those who were in the midst of a diagnosis; and others experiencing different kinds of trials in life. The blog led to Nadine's first book, *Hold On, Let Go: Facing ALS With Courage and Hope.*

As well as an author and blogger, Nadine is an education assistant and fitness instructor. She's a rock collector, a sunset chaser and (slightly obsessed) photo-taker. She's a cat person turned dog freak and a keen student of life, love and God. She's a mom, stepmom, grandma, sister, daughter, auntie, cousin, niece, friend and wife (again).

Nadine lives in Maple Ridge, B.C., Canada with her husband, Chris Ryan. They enjoy spending time with family, going for walks, bike rides and eating ice cream. They both have a heart for missions and are involved in the family ministry, Project Wellness. Project Wellness focuses on drilling wells and taking care of orphans in Malawi, Africa (projectwellness.ca). It's a division of Amazon Evangelism, the society Nadine's parents founded. Nadine is honoured to be vice president of the society.

Find Nadine's books and blog at nadinesands.com